Christianity
Churchianit

Finbar Doran

Table of Contents

Dedication

To the memory of my mother who was very brave and courageous, not letting other people's fears and ignorance stop her. It cost her a lot to do what's right. She truly had an understanding of the love of God. She was an inspiration for me.

John 12 v 24: Most assuredly, I say to you, unless a grain of wheat falls into the ground and dies, it remains alone, but if it dies, it produces much grain.

About the Author

Finbar Doran has been a Christian for twenty-five years and yet, his understanding of Christianity developed fully, only after a while of becoming a strict follower of Church. In his discovery of faith and love of God, he stumbled across the truth of life and the true meaning of Christianity.

Christianity or Churchianity? Is Finbar's first book, comprising of the experiences he had lived as a true Christian and not merely a follower of Church or what is known as Churchianity.

Preface

My name is Finbar Doran. I live in Northern Ireland and have been a Christian for twenty-five years. I am divorced with two young children. I had a difficult upbringing from my early childhood with losing my mother in tragic circumstances at an early age and being raised by different family members over the years which led me to feel I never belonged to anyone. Circumstances such as these made it difficult for me to connect with anyone, not even friends and love interests.

I was a champion boxer in my teens. In my early twenties, I decided to live abroad for three years working as a dancer in a club around Majorca and Tenerife. Ironically, this is where I first heard the gospel and got saved. God brought great changes in my life, but He seemed distant.

I experienced years of depression, self-pity and victim mentality with some faith but no love. I was not living the life of a Christian. To live life as a Christian, I needed to know the difference between what Christianity is and what it is not. To know what it is to walk with God more clearly and be more of the person I am made to be. I enjoy my prayer time a lot, and thankfully, my years of depression have come to an end. I have become more at peace with myself and others.

As a young person before my Christian faith, I always had a desire to do what is right, even if I was the only one. I always stood out and felt like "the oddball" at times over this, a little lonely. I had a love for the truth and being true to myself.

At 23 years of age, after becoming a Christian for a few months, I started to notice all in Church was not quite what it was in the Bible. I noticed double standards to what is right and wrong in the minds of people towards others. It was like somehow God must have double standards as they do. The biggest thing I noticed was repetitiveness in the prayer meetings.

God made a few changes in me after a few years as a Christian, and the biggest change was my prayer life. It became more powerful, joyful and real. It was and is the most satisfying thing—a thrill to my soul.

As the years went by, I discovered many things I had never expected to. I have been to many prayer meetings in big Churches and popular denominations, only to find sometimes I was the only one to turn up, besides if someone had to open the door. Yet I looked forward to the meetings so much. The whole point of the gospel is we can connect with God in Christ. Beautiful fellowship with God. Yet this is missing a lot in Church. They sing about Jesus, preach about Jesus and go around the world to teach about Jesus, but not many seem comfortable going to a prayer meeting (including the worship leaders and teachers) to meet with our Lord. In short, many seemed to be like lost souls in a prayer meeting, hoping not to be noticed or expected to pray. The prayers they prayed are the same prayers they are still praying twenty-five years later. My own praying felt depressing and repetitive, and I was terrified of praying out loud in a prayer meeting.

God has made big changes in me, and lately, private prayer is much more joyful. I am surprised at times how easy it is to hear from God in prayer after all prayer means to communicate. If you are not communicating then maybe you are not praying, you are just saying "prayers". Do people believe that God really wants to and will talk to them? Do we see prayer as an awe-inspiring moment to talk to the almighty God and our heavenly Father who loves us? Do we see it as something we need to force ourselves to do, just to keep an angry God happy? Or something we must perform well?

In this book, I have written about misunderstandings and beliefs that God's people have fallen into for thousands of years. Prayer and the love of God are major things, yet they are the most misunderstood, turning major things into minor, and minor things into major. Not to mention, it puts popular religious culture above the Bible. I also talk about what we should expect in our prayer life with God, and how real it should be.

Chapter 1

The Truth Can Be as Clear as Black and White, if Only We Have the Courage to See It

The term Churchianity came to me from God before I found out it was an actual word. Which one of these faiths do you believe and trust in? Do you know the difference? In short, Christianity is established on and centred upon Jesus Christ, in who He is and what He taught, as it is in the Bible. It appears to be very straight forward and simple, however, on the other hand, Churchianity is a broader term for different types of man's own version of Christianity, based on snippets from the Bible, with the remainder based on religious traditions and popular beliefs.

This directly affects the practice of our faith and prayer life. Much of the Bible is very transparent, apart from a few verses on prophecy and end of times. So as Christians, how do we know which one do we believe and trust in? This book will hopefully help to answer that. As quite simply, it can make the difference between going to heaven or hell, along with directly affecting our lives on earth. Further, I would say that a high percentage of believers who identify themselves as Christians are still being deceived by this counterfeit religion known as Churchianity. There are three fundamental reasons for Christians being deceived by the deception of Churchianity – fear, pride and lack of knowledge.

A person who attains more knowledge than others in one area of life can have pride that blinds them from their ignorance in other areas. Like knowing salvation comes through faith in the finished work of the Lord Jesus Christ alone, as we can't work our way into heaven. Knowing this truth is major, but it is not everything, it is more like the starting point of a walk with God, or at least it should be. Fear can blind us, as we can easily believe what we want to, being under pressure to fit in. We do not want to believe or even think differently from others that are close to us, such as our family members, friends or Church people, as we do not want to offend anyone, so 'going with the flow' is the easy option for us. This is why people can be easily deceived, as it makes life easier… But only for the moment, as it is easy to just follow the crowd. However, what people do not realise is that it is a lie in the long run, and above all things, we will have to give an account for our actions to God. Furthermore, we miss out on realising what our life's purpose is about. Sadly, it appears that too many people do not care about that, even people with the Christian faith, and at times myself, I might add.

We know of the religious Jews that Jesus rebuked. They were so passionate about some laws, that no one did anything on the Sabbath, that they did not want you to do.

They had no problem believing that some things were evil to put into their mouths. However, the same religious people did not seem to care very much about the life of others when they were in need of love in action, they were indeed very unpleasant, judgemental, self-righteous people, and had no real heart for the greatest commandments to love God with everything and our neighbours as ourselves. Of course, no Christian would like to think they are like that. Yet, this Churchianity is just a continuation of what the Jews did 2000 years ago.

I know that certain "Christians" locked children's play swings in the parks to stop children from playing on Sundays. They would be outside in large crowds complaining about people wanting to play football on Sundays. They would also be horrified if they thought that we smoked cigarettes or drank alcohol. Their understanding of God came more so from their own projections, and who they are before him, was based on popular opinion. All of this, of course, affected how they prayed and lived. Yet the question, whether they believe in the love of God or do they have love in their lives for others, was not even a question.

I wonder how many of the same "Christians" ever offered any help to the same people or showed love to those they had seen doing their own thing on a Sunday! Where were they when others were sick and in need? Where were they when others had no money? Both Christianity and

Churchianity have their main rules. With Christianity, it's, "You shall love God with all your heart, soul, mind and strength, and love your neighbour as yourself," which will affect our morals and every area of our lives. With Churchianity, it is, you shall not have sex until you're married, and you shall not smoke, drink or work on a Sunday. This will not affect our love for God and for others. This could make us worse off.

Jesus often spoke of the moral, religious Jews that did not work on Sabbath, and gave money to the temple, yet they would ignore the vulnerable and poor people on the street, while the unbeliever (the good Samaritan) would come along who more than likely was not so moral and religious, yet they had a love for the hurt and the needy, and a heart to help them even at his own cost. Who really is the most lost?

I remember walking miles to Church one morning in the rain, and I was drenched. As I was leaving Church afterwards, an older lady saw me. She told me I should not walk home in the rain. I told her I had no other way back home, and no one offered a lift, so I have to walk. Many people heard this, but all turned their backs to me with their Bibles under their arms. Sadly, I have too many stories like this. It was the early start of my understanding of Churchianity within the Church. Many other believers I have spoken to have told me similar stories, about how they were

4

ill and in the hospital with no people from their Church visiting them.

One story that stands out to me is about a man who told me he was a helper in Church for twenty-seven years. He had fallen ill with heart problems amongst other medical complications. He informed people from the Church that he was ill and would be in the hospital for a few months. Sadly, during this time, not one person from his Church visited him, yet his Church was popular with hell, fire and brimstone. Churchianity does not have Godly love as a priority; rather, it has moral pride; love your church denomination, do not ask questions, look religious and be more concerned with yourself looking religious. Last but not least, put your money in the basket. In Churchianity, to love others, they first have to tick many boxes and be just like them. Likewise, because of projections towards God, in Churchianity, to pray to God, they believe they must tick some boxes as well as faith in the name of Jesus. To them, what Jesus has done himself, it is too good to be true, and that alone was enough. They believe they must add to faith in Jesus!

It is just like Cain and Able, with two different offerings before God. Able was accepted, and Cain was rejected. Able's was based on the sacrifice of the animal, symbolic of Jesus's death, and Cain's was based on the fruits he had grown, symbolic of ignorant good intentions (dead works). In Churchianity, they try to come to God with both the offerings that are faith in Jesus, plus their good religious intentions. Usually, many misunderstandings came from a single Bible verse taken out of context. In the Bible, we read of Jewish people coming to the temple to pray with thanksgiving, and in the New Testament, we read about coming to God in prayer with thanksgiving.

Thanksgiving helps us in our faith, but it does not pave the way. Jesus alone is the way. I have given thanks with praise and worship for many years trying to get to God in prayer and get his favour in my life to no avail. Then God challenged me to come to him in faith alone in what Jesus did on my behalf as being enough. And I remember taking one step and believing at the same time I was in the Holies of Holies through faith in who I am in Christ. And for the first time in my life true thankfulness came out of me. Then I realised that thanksgiving and praise are not to get grace from God, but true thankfulness is because I already am in the grace of God in Christ. Thanks, does not make a way as Jesus himself is the way. Thanks, is just a good attitude to help us. Because when God loves us, there is grace. Grace is the result of God's love.

When I understood this, it totally changed my worship also. I was no more trying to worship like an orphan, with all my efforts to try and get something from God, while never having much peace in my heart.

I know many people who are trying to be accepted by God through worship and religious duties. Worship is about who God is, and thanks is about what he has done for us in Christ. Worship and praise are not a price we pay to get God to do something for us. I see them just as I was, trying so hard and giving God so much worship, yet having no peace or love for even themselves in their hearts.

Churchianity has brought these wrong beliefs into the Church. In Churchianity, a person says a prayer like an orphan to God as if they're begging. The believer begins to exhibit a victim mentality, to try to get God to do something, or at least to try to get God to want to do something. Basically, all about telling God what you want Him to do and saying it all in the name of Jesus at the end of it, to somehow send it like a text to God.

Churchianity prayers are repetitive, predictable, joyless and even performance. In Churchianity, people pray to God at a distance with no dependency on the Holy Spirit, and zero expectation of connecting or hearing from God. Churchianity is a disconnected faith from what is true, mostly praying for what is already with us in Christ. It is like asking for God to send His Spirit, asking God to give spiritual authority to Christians, asking God to be with His people. I even read a popular Christian post today saying, "Hope is on the way." Of course, I replied under it that hope is here.

Nearly everything that God has told us is here like his kingdom. The Church folk keep praying as if they are still waiting on it to happen. A little like the Jews waiting on the Messiah 2000 years ago and still are today. Likewise Church folk are looking for what has already happened and giving to Christians, 2000 years ago. If I believe hope is coming, in order to believe that I first must believe the lie that hope is not yet here.

I call Churchianity the disconnected gospel. While in Christianity the prayer is more about what God has already done for us in Christ, and in His name we will communicate as a child, to our Father and more often it is Him who tells us what we need to hear or do. I could count on my fingers how many people seem to pray as a Christian in Church. Yet, too often, all doors will be closed to these people in Church.

Biblical ignorance is one thing in a person who has never read the Bible, however, denial is a painful fact in that a person knows the truth, yet rejects the reality of the truth as it will cost them to follow it. People who choose to be 'ignorant' tend to believe in what religious beliefs they grew up with or following whatever was popular at the time. Therefore, I believe that some Christians with this mindset, struggle with the ability to think critically, to be able to think for themselves and to follow it through. This takes courage as the majority of people will think you are wrong. We, as Christians, do not want to be known as 'sheep following sheep' rather we should be following the shepherd. Sadly, this is not always the case.

Christianity is not up for man to change it into what he wants. If man makes his own version of Christianity, I call that Churchianity as both of these have different beliefs and values. With Christianity, main things are love, joy and peace. With Churchianity, it's don't smoke, and drink and serve your church. Joy is very important in Christianity. As the bible says, "The joy of the Lord is our strength. And in his presence is fullness of Joy and pleasures at his right hand." And as Peter says, "With God there is joy unspeakable and full of glory. But in Churchianity there is no joy to speak of. There is only gloom. Joy is not only unacceptable in Churchianity, it is also seen as disrespectful. But that's because in Churchianity they take themselves too serious instead of having serious sentiment for God. In Christianity, we are not supposed to take ourselves too seriously, but take God seriously. When it comes down to it, if we are honouring God and his covenant as the Bible says, then we will be joyful in the house of prayer.

In Christianity, there is freedom and liberty, in Churchianity followers are uptight and self-conscious. Christianity gives joy, Churchianity kills joy. Don't let anyone rob you of what Jesus Christ paid for you to have. In Christianity, you are more than a conqueror, a king and priest in Christ, accepted in the beloved. In Churchianity, you are nothing but a lowly beggar and guilty sinner. You can't believe both. Jesus warns us about the lies of the religious leaders. Poison will kill alone, and it will also kill if put in a healthy meal.

Likewise, I know of many believers that think they are walking in truth, yet they come out with the poison of false humility and lies they get from the Church. It's so important for people not to be so gullible to believe everything they hear. You must read the Bible yourselves. You can't believe and pray as a follower of Churchianity and get Christian results. Christianity believes the good news, Churchianity believes in good intentions. Check who you truly believe and follow.

Chapter 2

Sheep follow their herd 99% of the time, even into the dark.

Yet I dare to walk the lonely path followed generally by 1%. I have experienced many situations of 'willful ignorance' throughout my life; however, the most prominent one that I witnessed was in the early nineties. I was not a Christian at that time, but this is an example of how people are easily misled and my courage to do what is right even when I am alone. I was attending a rock concert in Dublin where the stadium had around ten thousand people capacity. Stupidly, I consumed too much alcohol that evening and became sick on the bus on my way to the concert. I was abruptly woken by the bus driver when I arrived. As I got off the bus, it was evident that many of the thousands of others had arrived earlier and were waiting to get into the stadium at the back of the building. However, rather than just following the crowds, my critical thinking is too often a fault finder. I could clearly see there were no lights in the area where the others were standing as it was dark, plus the door was closed, and no-one was getting in. However, I could see the lights on the side of the building. Therefore, thinking for myself, I gazed around and noticed that there was a pathway with a mobile fence put up on each side with street lights on each side, and a sign on a pole with an arrow pointing, clearly stating *'the way in'* in clear black and white. How could others did not see clearly, what was as clear as three pink elephants to me? Because of willful ignorance, others did not realise or care about what was so clear to notice that they followed blindly what was popular rather than what was correct.

As I stood there, I noticed two girls walking by me to join the rest of the crowd. I politely told them that they were walking in the wrong direction! However, they ignored me and looked at me as if I was crazy. Even though with all the evidence in front of them, they still decided to follow the crowd because everyone else was doing it. I know ignorance far too well and how it works, and yes, I will admit I was sick from consuming too much alcohol on the bus, but yet none of this changes the truth about the correct way into the stadium to see their rock band. As I slowly made my way into the stadium, I remember thoughts entering my head saying to me, "Do you think everyone else is wrong and you are right?" I could even feel intense pressure from that thought, so much so that for a few seconds, I did turn to follow the 99%, but then it was not in me to live in denial of the truth to follow the willful ignorance. How can I walk from light and truth to be with the many in the lost darkness? So, I turn back to the right way and thought someday this step of courage will prove worthwhile and rewarding. I remember shouting at them, *"You are all going the wrong way and that is not my opinion as it is written here on the sign"*. But truth and evidence are not enough for the majority of people. I later noticed the concert officials telling many revellers that they were in the wrong way. Just a few minutes before, I was the crazy lost loner who was far behind to the nine thousand nine hundred and ninety-nine of the reveller's eyes. However, a few minutes later, their ignorance was replaced by the knowledge of knowing the correct way into the stadium. I went from looking stupid and behind many to being smart and in front. I remember thinking to myself, if I were to ask each person here one by one, *"Are you a free thinker who's honest with yourself to think are doing what's right and true, or do you just follow what's popular regardless if it's right or wrong, so long as you just fit in"?* I would so easily assume that one after the other would say they are an honest, free thinker and not an ignorant person who just follows the crowd. Yet the overwhelming evidence tells the different. I have witnessed many experiences of this behaviour all my life, as the majority of people go one way and myself going the other. I, at times, get honoured as the only correct among the crowd.

Chapter 3

More sheep following sheep 99%. I dare
again to be true and amongst the 1%.

I was in an assembly class at my school. The headteacher asked everyone to do something that was so very easy to do, and most, including the other teachers, did not. I was sure one hundred per cent that next time he would ask us, no one else would do. Ninety-nine per cent of people only seem to do what is popular. I made a conscious effort to do as the headteacher said, and of course, he did ask us to do the simple thing again. It was only me in the school that did, as he asked. He pointed me out and said, "Finbar was the only person to do as I said". Yet if I were to ask them all, "Do you think honestly for yourself, or are the sheep of the herd that follows other sheep"? I am sure they all would like to think. They do think for themselves and not just ignorantly follow the crowd. However, the evidence shows otherwise. An ignorant person will have an ignorant defence. They will say, "But everyone else is like this and do it, including the teachers who are qualified, more experienced, and get paid to do their job. They were in unity with the ninety-nine per cent. I know this, and I am not ignorant of their ignorance. They just do not realise, but the fact is what was said by the headteacher. I am not saying I am a better person, but where I am strong, I am bound to help where others are weak.

Clearly, many other's weakness is doing what's popular rather than what is right. Just as many seem to be so connected with others that they cannot seem to give attention to anything beyond that or outside of their bubble. People want to make something of their lives but do not want to lose some connections with ninety-nine per cent. As the people in the business world know this, but without Jesus, they may have some levels of success, yet will still be lost. They may be following 1% of people but are not following Jesus. The point of this story is to let people know that they need not just follow the crowd and believe what is popular, even if it is in a church.

If we think about it and do what is right or to think for ourselves, it can sometimes leave us in a zone of loneliness. The truth is loneliness is the price one has to pay at times. Loneliness has been the hardest part of my life. A few times, it has been rewarding to do right and not follow popular ignorant notion, but sadly very few, to be honest. Like that day at the rock concert with ten thousand people attending, who would the revellers hate most? The answer is *me*, the one telling them they were going the wrong way. These revellers are all in agreement with each other and see no fault in them because of their ignorance. Then there is me, the loner, telling everyone that they are all going the wrong way. No-one likes to be told they are wrong. I used to think to myself, I would see fault in no-one, and I would fit right in with no disagreements. If only I was ignorant as well, weak to think for myself, or was willing to live in denial of the clear truth, then my life would be much easier in several ways.

In my prayer for comfort to God, I was reminded of John in the Bible, who was deserted on an island where he used to write books. Many of the Apostles wrote their books when they were alone in prison. John Bunyan, who was a great Christian and a free thinker, was imprisoned with persecution from the people of the "Church", or should I say people from the religion of Churchianity. John Bunyan was put in prison merely for being an honest Christian as well as living, praying, and preaching Christianity.

Many church folks admire and regard Martin Luther King as a great man who was also regarded as a free thinker. He looked at what the Bible said rather than popular tradition. I am sure many have read the same bible verses as him. However, they appear to value tradition much more than the Bible itself. Martin Luther became dissatisfied with the dead tradition, and therefore it was easier for people to believe in the truth. Moreover, what was a man's tradition doing for his life? - very little. More importantly, what could it do for his soul in front of God? - Nothing. There is a fear of not being in agreement with others, as it can ultimately cost something or the other. Others will judge us according to their ignorance, but God will judge us according to his words. And just like there was a reformation 500 years ago, I believe the Church could do again with one. My biggest advice would be for folks to open their Bible and read it. Do not take in everything that we hear from the pulpit. I just heard a preacher say that if you want to know someone's relationship with God, just look at their prayers in life. A point to ponder, I must say.

'Churchianity' is similar to the false version of the Jewish faith over 2000 years ago. This false doctrine has placed religious traditions of man before the Bible. As Jesus pointed out in Mark chapter 4, verse 7-9, "And in vain they worship me, teaching as doctrines - the commandments of men. For laying aside the commandments of God, you hold the tradition of men, the washing of pitchers and cups, and many other such things you do." He said to them, "All too well reject the commandment of God, that you may keep tradition". The next few verses after this, Jesus describes to them in an example of the Bible saying one thing and their tradition displaying another. They will reject what the Bible says in order to preserve a tradition. This is so clear in the Bible, yet a very high percentage of people who claim to believe this still follow it. However, they will not admit this or at least do not realise it. The reason for this is denial or just ignorance. After the fall of Adam and Eve to sin, the first reaction was denial. It was not consuming alcohol, smoking, or even lust. It was denial. They were afraid, to be honest, about things and tried to pass the blame. Denial is the fear of facing the consequences of being honest. Yet, in my twenty-odd years being a Christian, I cannot remember a time that denial has ever been preached in Church. That speaks volumes in itself. Additionally, I would say it is more of an epidemic. If no one confronts a problem in a church, then it will have its way for spread without hindrance. It would take a brave Church leader to confront these issues, not only with his congregation but within himself too. Another example of false doctrine is that it will use the most important attributes within the Bible and make them seem insignificant. This will cause things to be taken easily out of context. All these wrong changes in faith don't happen overnight, but subtly over time. Love seemed to be a distant thing that was not talked about or understood much. A lot of confusion about what love actually is?

Chapter 4

Faith, morals and doctrine are not much of the good without love.

A major ignorance in priorities now within the Church appears to be the same problem that Jesus had when he rebuked the Jews over 2000 years ago. Jesus said in Luke chapter 11, Verse 42, "But woe to you Pharisees! For you tithe mint and rue and all manner of herbs, and pass by justice and the love of God. These you ought to have done, without leaving the others undone". Yet until this day, giving ten per cent of the money is talked about so frequently in Churches. It is discussed so much as though our lives depend upon it. However, some Christians may not have a love for themselves or others or even truly believe that we are loved by God. In Church that will not even be a problem so long as you do not do something outwardly wrong. How many Christians within the Church are feeling empty of love whilst putting money in the basket, hoping that somehow God might bail them out of their despair and sadness. Or at least let them keep his good books. How many Christians have been generously giving money because the preacher emphasised it to be a major thing before God to get his help? Yet the givers see very little of the blessing or even none of the blessings that the preachers talked about. We have given it time, and yet even decades go by with generous money

19

being given to the Church as a top priority. Yet Christians are still living without much sign of God's blessings or closeness in their life. Whereas the love of God is rarely spoken about.

I recall my first fifteen years as a Christian and have calculated five times that I have heard a sermon preached on the love of God. That works out to be one occasion every three years on average that the love of God was preached about in Church. I might add that I was attending the best Churches, known for having the greatest teachings, as an old saying goes – *the best of a bad bunch*. This does not mean that those people were bad Christians, but they have been raised with the same mentality. Yet when we read the Bible, we can clearly see Jesus constantly speaking about the two main commandments – 'To love God with all your heart, all your soul, all your mind, and all your strength' and 'love your neighbour as you love yourself'. However, how many believers are there that gives money to the Church, have good morals, do not work on a Sunday, and do not smoke or drink but have very little love for others outside of their box or even for themselves? You would assume that after two thousand years, we would have got it right in the Church by now, however, I admit, I myself was this person for many years. I generously gave quite frequently to the Church. I tried to be as moral as I could, yet I led a miserable life and remained unemployed for ten years. Doesn't that sound like the blessing of God? But I thank God, his word is true, and he answers things in context. 1 Corinthians chapter 13, verse 3 states, "And though I bestow all my goods to feed the poor, and though I give my body to be burned, but have not to love, it profits me nothing". This verse clearly says that without love, your giving has **NO PROFIT**. Even if you were to suffer because you gave so much, you still do not profit. I doubt you will ever hear a minister tell his people that you are wasting your time and money if you are giving money and do not have pure intentions and love. The question is, do you have love? They did not ask because you do not love God enough, as I am sure we all could love God more. I have always had a problem with love and my years as being a Christian. The first words that came out of my mouth after becoming a Christian were "I love you" to the men that prayed for me that day. But after that, love was something that I would feel very little or understood in the true sense. No wonder I was easily depressed in my life. How could I be in love while at the same time, be against it? There is a Bible verse that says, "people are lovers of themselves rather than lovers of God". I took that as though it was evil to love myself, so to hate myself or at least not love myself seemed the best thing in Churchianity. To speak little of myself seemed like humility. But as I will explain in this book later, how the dangers of taking a Bible verse out of context can have a crippling effect on your life, and it did play havoc on my life. As the world seems to have a bad version of self-love, that the Church rejected, anything to do with having a love for self - altogether.

According to the New-Age movement, self-love is number one in their beliefs according to them. But in Christianity–to love for God, because New-Age and other folks teach on self-love. Somehow Christians have thrown the baby out with the bathwater and have rejected loving ourselves because ignorant folk do that. As at that time, I did not have any love for myself. I was very harsh at times with people and even with my own children. I attended church weekly, read my Bible daily, and I prayed every day, yet no love. My life was horrible. I became angry quite easily, and I felt like a forgotten orphan. Loneliness was horrible. In one way, I knew this loneliness happens for becoming a free thinker. However, more so as with no self-love, it meant that I didn't have peace within myself either. But thankfully, God helped me in my despair. After speaking badly to my kids one day, mainly my son, who caused problems in our relationship and still to this day, my children, unfortunately, have not got totally over it years later.

I knew my good morals, such as giving money to Church, no smoking or drinking, and other good things, did not help. Truth be told, the more moral I became, the more miserable and angrier I became. Sometimes I was not so moral, and I dated a few women, which made me feel better, or so I thought. By dating women, I was at least feeling some kind of connection and even valued. However, I knew it was not the best thing to do in the long run. My real help came one day in prayer when God let me know that insecurity will destroy my life and relationships if I let it, even though it is not God's will. I had only one choice. I had to learn to love myself as myself. I tried to take in the main truth many times that God loves me, but it would not sink in, at least not for me. I even had a mighty experience of the love of God one day in a Church. Yet I left the Church the same way that I came in. Why? Because I experienced it, but I never really believed it. To believe is the key, but God knew as long as I did not love myself as myself. I would not believe in the past that others love me, including God. God explained to me how to love myself so simply that I was amazed. It became clear to me that loving myself as myself had nothing to do with the world's love based on material and physical things like looks, fame, and fortune. It had nothing to do with how I even performed as a Christian but in order to love myself because God loves me, and he commands me to love myself. I sat back on my chair and said for the first time in my life, "I LOVE ME AND GOD LOVES ME". I kept repeating these beautiful words to myself and in a Godly meditation. I reflected on what I was saying and believed it. There was some resistance at the start, by having negative thoughts which had held me captive throughout my life, saying- "You

23

cannot love yourself as you do not deserve it". With a few other foolish reasons lurking in my mind. However, I rejected these thoughts, which were causing me to reject myself and others around me during my whole life. I even had to change my wrong beliefs based on one Bible verse, in which I took it totally out of context, saying people will be lovers of themselves rather than lovers of God. I took that verse wrongly, believing that it must be bad to love myself.

It was a beautiful meditation, and I knew it was like medication to the mind and soul. I had to remember that, and when the lonely forgotten orphan thoughts and feelings would surface, I knew it was time to tell myself I am loved by God, and I love myself. In the last part of John 15:10, Jesus said to abide in his love. May we do that more in prayers. Sadly, I have yet to hear a sermon on this important subject. A few days later, after taking this all in that as I was walking, I could feel something in my head changing. It felt as though my brain was rewiring itself. The pressure was moving off me so much that I began to feel extremely relaxed. It was like I smoked cannabis back in my youth. I remember God telling me not to worry as I will balance out from feeling overly calm since it is just my brain getting used to the change. I found it easier to love others and have a love for myself. Even more importantly, I wholeheartedly believed that God loved me more, which helped me to love him more.

How can we bear the fruits of the spirit like patience, kindness, gentleness, and much more without love itself? That is like wanting to eat an omelette without the eggs. My life circumstances began to change after a few months when I finally found employment after many years. I was also given my first car. All of these gifts and opportunities were given to me within one week. It was the biggest change in my life after salvation. Some like myself believed in fear of God, just not his love as much. I say all of these things to show the dangers of leaving out the most important things while giving so much emphasis to lesser things. Additionally, this is to explain that we can so easily be limited one way or the other in life because of ignorance, lack of knowledge also. We all have blind spots in our own lives, and therefore we should have mercy on others. As pride blinds us, humility helps us to see more clearly. Love is the key to help with that. You may have faith for this and that, but Galatians 5: 6 reads..., "but faith working through love". Therefore, if you want your faith to work, then you need love. Without genuine Godly love, we will easily love the wrong things, which is why we can have some addictions. People just think of drug or porn addiction. But the addiction for praise and approval seems to go unnoticed. With these addictions comes the pressure to perform.

Chapter 5
Good leadership is crucial for a good prayer meeting.

When a minister or a Church leader is going to pray, do they show what it is like to connect with God? Do they come across as some formula prayers that predictable? Some formula prayers can be ok at some specific times, but if it is heard nearly by all people, then it is harder for others to learn prayer. Therefore, in prayer meetings, a few leaders like to take control and not let others have a chance. One reason is they do not have much faith in how their congregation will pray (even though they taught them!!)? Plus, a person may come into a prayer meeting and make a scene by doing something to bring everybody's attention towards themselves.

The Bible says, know that labour among you. If someone is new to a Church, they should show respect and get to know others. Be known before, even thinking about trying to be seen or take part in some things. I heard of a time when a woman comes in during prayer. She runs around making a scene breathing heavily, got up on the stage and fell to the floor. A good leader should stop that behaviour and make it clear that prayer is not about drawing attention to oneself or do something needlessly. Yet to stop others from getting an opportunity to pray because of fear. This can get out of hands which is not a good thing either. Maybe have a rule in a prayer meeting of getting to know people or permission from leaders before praying openly in a prayer meeting. This will help keep things in order. Also, making sure they can pray in a local language that all may understand, as it is not only common sense, but Paul also teaches about how praying in a language that others will understand when in public. That is one reason why prayer meetings are best with people you know and smaller groups. Jesus did this. I see a good leader as a referee in football. They are not there to kick the ball by themselves but to let others do it while keeping an eye on them that it is done according to the rules. Any wrongdoing will bring a warning for them or even sent off the field straight away. Likewise, Church leaders should also trust their congregation to pray. After all, they taught them how to pray. Respect for God and his word needs to be restored in our lives. The pressure to perform in prayer comes from a lack of fear and love for God, compared to the fear and love for the others that are listening.

If we try to serve two masters in prayer, we will not have that connection with any God. Rather just try to perform or trust in the formula prayer. To stop this religious nonsense, we need to admit our weaknesses and sins before God to repent and admit our lack of love towards God. I admitted to God at times in the past that praying was boring to me. God already knows us and still loves us; how can he help or heal us? If we won't be honest with ourselves and God. Prayer is

27

not about us trying to perform, but it's about his amazing grace towards us in the shape of Christ. The Lord will only put new wine into new wineskins, time for believers to throw away the old formula performance wineskins and put on the wineskin of Christ in us, and us in him. When Jesus taught, he did it in front of thousands, but normally in times of prayer, it was him with the twelve and sometimes with just a few. These examples should be applied in the Church with smaller groups praying and all with more of a chance to take part. Also, at times when Jesus went to pray for some, he first put people out of the room who did a lot of crying but had not got faith in what the Lord was going to do. So, we see that who is in the room will have an effect on a person who is praying. When a person is praying, he can discern if the people have faith or not. At times in the Bible, we read of the disciples seeing that people had faith to be healed. So, faith and unbelief can be discerned. At times I have prayed with a few, and I could tell easily who had faith and hunger for the Lord? It would make it so much easier to pray when we are with people of faith. I also remember praying among a few hundred believers. They mentioned a request for prayer for someone who was ill. After many long prayers of tears with old English language and a reverend tone to the voices taking turns in either begging God or telling him what to do with sounds of approval after each prayer. I had the audacity to have faith in the biblical truths and pray as a

Christian and mention that person's name in a short prayer. I prayed, "in the name of Jesus Christ be healed". I could have heard a pin drop in the room, and I felt so out of place praying as a Christian in a church. And I never discerned any faith there and realised why Jesus put some people out of the room before he prayed. It would have been better for me if I went to a pub and prayed alone in the toilet as there would not have been religious ignorance, resisting me praying even though I did it as taught in the Bible. So as harsh as it may sound, there needs to be a clear vision again from the Bible, as to how to pray and ask God to show us when we are drifting off course. Praying as a Christian should be the norm in a church and not something strange or unusual.

I attended a relative's wedding who were of the Catholic denomination and various others. They asked me to say grace for the food served. I also prayed a word of knowledge to the married couple and felt a little excited in prayer. A part of me thought, they will grab me and throw me out of the room, after all, not all believers like how I prayed, so what would happen here. But as soon as I sat down, they all started to clap since they loved how I prayed. I laughed as they clapped because I was relieved. They did not throw me out as the fear had made them lied and said that they would. Now thinking about it, I see my Christian prayer was more welcomed in a room with people drinking and smoking than in a church. Probably because they did not see me as a threat.

Our time with God is so important. So how we pray is also important. Telling people how not to pray is also important since Jesus did this. But in the name of being nice, people are not corrected about prayer. In the name of being nice, many people are living in ignorance as people do not want to hurt their feelings with the truth. We are even told in the Bible to let a person know that they will receive nothing of the Lord in prayer, James 1:7. *Prayer is probably the biggest indicator of what is going on in a person's beliefs and life. Prayer has been so misunderstood and disconnected from God for so long that it does not seem to be a problem. As people have been raised this way, 99% see it as normal.*

Before I was a Christian (though I thought I was because I believed in God), I used to say prayers and put – in Jesus name at the end of whenever I was a lost soul. The thing that sets apart Christianity from other faiths is that we can connect with God in prayer. As a Christian, to just settle for saying prayers and hoping for the best is to be easily robbed from what Jesus died for us to have. Before the fall, Adam walked with God. After the fall, mankind lost that connection. The whole point, when Jesus came and did, all he did was to restore that connection. Faith comes by hearing the word of God. We can and should read it. But Jesus said *my sheep hear my voice, and they follow me, and the place that normally happens is during prayer.* Why do people think it is so difficult for us to hear from God!!? After all, his word is powerful enough to create the heavens and the earth. Remember, only one Jewish priest could go to the Holies of Holies one time a year which was where a divine connection existed with God, and the priest heard from God himself. Yet our Lord Jesus Christ paid the price for us all to be worthy enough in him and his name to go to that perfect place of prayer. Where we can hear from God also and know his nearness. After all, what kind of a father does not want to talk to his children? How we see God can affect our faith to hear from him.

Chapter 6

Wrong ways to measure. A root of ignorance.

In explaining how wilful ignorance works, here goes its explanation. People who are 'ignorant' use the wrong instruments to measure something, for example – would you use a stop watch to measure the length of your house? Of course not, you would use a measuring tape. Would you use a measuring tape to find out how long it takes for you to run the length of the house? Of course not, you would use a stop watch. And while measuring weight, we do not use a stop watch or a measuring tape, rather we would use scales. You would think no one would be so foolish to use the wrong gadget to measure something just to check, whether it is right or wrong. Yet, it is probably the most prevalent way that people think in many areas of their life. To see if something is right or wrong, rather than go look and check for themselves using the proper measuring rules, they follow the crowd properly and honestly. It is the number one measuring rule to the ignorant. It is to believe if it is popular, then it must be right. If a Church minister says it or most people in Church believe it, it's got to be right, regardless of what the Bible says.

There is also another extreme when a person can think that he or she is always right, no matter what.

The Bible says in Proverbs **26:12**

"A person who is right in their own opinion. There's more hope for a fool than for him."

Therefore, when a person thinks different from the crowd, they can be easily mistaken, for this person is wise just in their own eyes. This kind of thinking sadly seems to go unnoticed. So much so, that when this person becomes a Christian, they think the same way. They go from one kind of bad thinking to another. Truth sometimes, seems to be harder for a free thinker as a Christian. You want to be a "good person", go to Church, sing your songs, hear a sermon, put money in the box, and go home. It is okay to have good morals, do not smoke or drink, no working on Sunday unless for healthcare, do not be different, but be a clone or a good servant. However, the question of do you have love in your life? Will not be asked. Nonetheless, it is not just their own fault, as they were raised with wrong thinking and wrong priorities.

Chapter 7

Moral people with little love. And not so moral yet with more love.

I have worked at many Christian houses especially building or doing other work for days at a stretch, during hot summer days. Yet they would hardly offer you a glass of water. They have Christianity related pictures placed around their houses and they would boast that they do not drink or smoke! However, I have been to houses of unbelievers, and it is quite hard to get them to stop making tea and coffee. As a biker, I have met non-Christian bikers who would go out of their way to help me when my motorbike broke down on the highway. I was shocked, after meeting them. I believed the Lord wanted me to teach them something and I hope that I did, but it was me actually learning from them as well. Looking back myself working in people's gardens, doing hard labour under the sun. I remember certain "believers" boasting about, how high in regard they were in their Church amongst others. However, what they can't see the ignorance and lack of love as the blind fold of Churchianity over the eyes of their minds saying, "I do not drink or smoke (publicly) and have sexual morals. I keep Sunday off work, and I give ten percent of my money to Church". That seems to be all that matters to them in a nutshell. Yet very little hospitality or never offered a sip of water even. Again, I admit I was like this as well too often, just like the fake faith was about two thousand years ago. They were very harsh about the Sabbath, they condemned the eating and drinking of things and hated anyone who failed in their sexual morals. Infact, they became passionate about stoning them to death. However, their love for themselves, God or others was not seen much. Much of this is what sounds like Christianity today, or should I say Churchianity being disguised as Christianity. Sadly, it is what people see in the Church. The blindness protrudes over people because they think they love God if they tick a few moral boxes and do what their Church leader says without question. And because love casts out fear, there is so little love that fear is the normal in church, and I mean crippling fear.

How can this be? And what is missing in "believers"? It is the lack of courage. Being a coward seems to be the popular unnoticed sin within the Church. In all of the times of my life where I went alone it took one thing, and that was to be courageous. Morals or wisdom will not do it, nor experience or knowledge but, being a coward in Church and life, makes it easy for you to be manipulated and controlled. There were many Jews who believed in Jesus as Lord two thousand years ago who were in religious connections, but they were afraid to give Jesus the honour that he was worthy of because they were a coward, they compromised, and denied publicly what they truly believed. Still, it seems to be okay to many in Church to "play it safe and be nice" but too often this could be cowardly. Just like a homosexual will say he is gay, and the thief will say he is an opportunist, the coward will say he is just being nice. One hundred percent of the Church will seemingly say and believe that murderers, liars and sexual sinners will go to hell if they do not repent, yet the same Bible says that neither the coward will enter the kingdom of God.

Revelation 21:8

"But the cowardly, the unbelieving, the vile, the murderers, the sexually immoral, those who practice magic arts, the idolaters and all liars-they will be consigned to the fiery lake of burning sulphur. This is the second death."

Sadly, being a coward is not only accepted in Church, it appears to be wanted in some as these people will be easily controlled. It is one thing to have approval of men, but that does not mean that we have God's approval. However, Churchianity loves the timid COWard. I place the letters COW highlighted on coward, as it reminds me how to explain, how a person can become a coward in Church. A young male cow (bull) gets castrated, by cutting off their testicles. This is done to the bull so it will not grow up to be as strong and also not let others take advantage of him easily. A bull with no testicles will not produce the hormone that causes it to grow big, strong, and even dangerous. It will also not be able to breed with other cows and be fruitful of itself. Additionally, it will be easily submissive and will be moved by farmers until they use them by selling them to the meat market. It is most likely where the term "you haven't got the balls" comes from. Relating it to Church, this is how Churchianity will try to do with the men's heart attending the Church. It will try to take masculinity from their heart by misuse of certain Bible verses such as Hebrews 13: 17

"Obey them that have rule over you and submit yourselves: for they watch for your souls."

Yet, somehow this seems to be taken in a way that no one is okay to disagree or want to think differently. In context, the Apostle Paul says in Galatians1:8

"But even if we, or an angel from heaven, preach any other gospel to you than what we preached to you, let him be accursed".

These are very strong words from Paul, which gives me permission as a Christian that I do not have to believe and do everything I am told, even in Church. I am allowed to have my own mind and I do not have to walk on eggshells, but as it is popular 'not to question or even doubt what Churches preach', therefore it is accepted as being right. If a man gives into honouring religious traditions, or even Church leadership above honouring God and his word, it is the same as a young bull having his testicles cut off. Only sadly a young bull gets this done by force while men let this happen to their hearts. A young bull will be trapped in a small cage, where it becomes hard for the bull to move with no momentum and easy for the former who just want to use the bull for his own selfish agenda and castrate it. So, likewise men in a Church can feel pressured into becoming just their servant, who are very predictable, unsure of themselves, timid and gentle...too gentle. Followers of the Church, more than followers of Christ. It almost feels like their masculinity has been broken. A high percentage of fellow believers I come across are very timid, weak, insecure, and surprisingly afraid of women. I know this as I myself lived like this in Church for years. Yet when I was in the world of bikers, they seemed anything but timid, weak, and insecure. I am certain we all have different fears but the lack of masculinity and men of courage in Church unspoken of, or even highlighted as a problem. Hopefully, this book can help folks to wake up and think, be responsible, and be a man. I ensure by God's grace not to let others castrate their heart.

Chapter 8

Example of honouring tradition more than the Bible. Yet I dare not.

I remember earlier in my faith, how I started to appreciate the Bible teaching much more as I read it daily. I could clearly see that the same Bible says, 'call no man your Father'. It is also the same Bible that says, 'call no man your teacher', For one is your father God in heaven and one is your teacher, the Christ, and you are ALL brethren - Matthew 23: 7 – 10. "Churches would know not to call a man father, yet at the same time they would call their own leaders titles before their first name."

The Bible says, "For you are all Brethren". Just like the sign I read at the concert the way in. What part of you are all brethren do people not understand? People without realising it, have believed in a God of double standards who is made in their own image with projections of themselves. Yet both have the same argument and answer to try to justify a title before the first name. When I asked someone from the Catholic denomination, 'why do you call a man father? Even though Jesus said call no man father, they say, Paul the apostle said he was a father to people he was writing to, plus it is to show respect to leaders. Yet when I have asked a church member 'why do you add titles before calling the first name?' They would reply with the same answer, even using the same out of context Bible verse about Paul saying, he was a father to people, just to justify doing with what Jesus clearly said not to do. And a contradict to how the apostles themselves spoke. When you have a vision of God that comes from your own projection, you are in trouble; for example, thinking God has one rule for some people and another rule for others, just as with titles to names, as with many other practices. Another example which I once heard a famous man having his own lifestyle saying that he believes Jesus was just like him. The BBible states who Jesus is rather than forming our own opinion. Read your Bible.

Chapter 9
Titles before names again.

If you have read the first few verses in most New Testament Bibles, you will read that ALL of them have called themselves by their first names, and other Church leaders by their first name, and not one of them have called the other Father, Pastor, Bishop before their first name. And this was verse after verse, chapter after chapter and book after book, but they gave honour to the names of the God and father of our Lord Jesus Christ. However, this evidence is not enough; as long as they are going along with the 99%, they think it must be right or at least okay. One way is Biblical, and the other way is popular. I am sure you can guess what stand I took.

I remember saying to a church leader that I had just learned this in the Bible, therefore, I will not call any brother in the Lord with a title before their first name. I was told "DON'T YOU DARE". I could feel the pressure, and I knew there was going to be a price to pay if I did not submit. I had a choice, to let them either castrate in my heart and become the "nice boy" or dare to say no to the pressure and be a man. This of course was challenging. I prayed about it and remember talking to God that I do not want the Church to think I am being disrespectful, but I do not want to live in denial of what the Bible so very clearly says in context. God reminded me of all the times that I went one direction and everyone else the other direction at the written or spoken word of man – and I was proven right. God challenged me several times in analyzing how much more important it is to go in the direction of the written or spoken word of God, even if or when the 99% of the "believers" were going the other way. I have some problems and weaknesses in my personality, but denial was never much of a problem. God reminded me, that during my times of loneliness, when I will not matter much to people and they will not always be with me, but rather God will always care and be with me. That thought made it easier for me to honour God more than man. Why does not every believer do that you may ask? FEAR is a simple answer, being the coward. I will give an example. There was a Church cult many years ago, and the leader was very much of an insecure control freak. He came across as loving and caring, but he became more insecure. They went to an island, and when trouble was coming, a few people dared to report him as he had changed for the worse. He asked them ALL to take medication which would kill them. After all, he was their Church leader, and the Bible says obey them that rule over you! Yet ninety nine percent of the people took the tablets and died. Why did they so easily submit to such vile evil? And use a Bible verse completely out of context, even to their own death you may ask? Because the Church leader told his right-hand men to shoot anyone who did not obey his leadership. There was a target on anyone's back who did not submit. There was a very small percentage of people whom "rebelled him" and ran, but sadly a few of them were killed, with a few surviving. They were going to die anyway, so either die as an obedient slave to man, or die as a free man. Ofcourse no average Church has guns pointing at people to shoot them if they do not completely submit to everything without question, but dare to be genuine about the word of God, let God be your leader, and see what happens. Dare to honour God above them. Do not be surprised if you feel you have a target on you or be seen as a trouble maker wanting to cause division. A person like myself will be seen as a troublemaker, and will be kept outside of the accepted box. I remember, God letting me know twenty-two years ago that if I compromise to please man, that life would be easy and I would fit right in, but I will not grow to who I am to be, and I will not do what I am created to do. However, if I dare to man up and honour God above the Church leadership, (yet still giving honour that is due to leadership) then it will be a difficult path for me, and I will be misunderstood or even rejected by my fellow believers. But in the long run it will pay off. I was hoping that the long run would only be a few months later. I thought to myself, how would a person be, think or pray to God if they read the Bible for what is says and loses the religious junk that it does not say, and didn't give into pressure to have performance prayers? This became quite an adventure in my life, but mainly my prayer life. It changed me so much that I stood out like an ugly duckling, and mainly during prayer meetings. God is who he says he is. He will do what he said he will do. I am who God says I am, and by his grace I will do what he said I will do. One thing is true, if we have our own made- up Jesus or have a wrong view of him, then we will be dry in our faith and prayers. Jesus said, John 7:38: "He who believes in me, as the scripture has said, out of his heart will flow rivers of living water."

We can ask ourselves, does the living water flow in us even when we pray as a Christian? Or is it too often just good intentions trying our best in Churchianity. We need to believe in Jesus according to the scripture, and not our own ideas. Just like how to meet with God in prayer, with a glad heart in faith as the Bible teaches us. Rather than our own religious ideas of being doom and gloom victim mentality, hoping to make God want to answer more. Without faith, it is impossible to please God.

I recall chatting to a Church leader, who was well respected in other countries as well. I chatted with him about what God will do in the last days from the Bible. He said God will not do that! I gave him the benefit of the doubt and showed him the Bible verse regarding the end times. After seeing this, he still said God would not do it. Why? Because the picture of God in the Bible went against his own religious beliefs. The picture he has of God, from his own projections is what is important to him, than who God is in the Bible, which did not mean so much. Still until this day, he is highly regarded and respected Evangelical leader. Why!? He is a nice man and wears a shirt and tie, and of course he doesn't smoke or drink! A reminder not to believe everyone's view of who God is.

Chapter 10

God says what he means and means what he says, so should you.

God speaks, but if he tells us, "Do not cast pearls before swine because they will trample over them." Mathew 7:6

From that and many more verses, we know that God will not be heard much by a person who either does not believe or just is not willing to obey his word. If we are faithful a little, then he will trust us with more.

Luke 16:10. Why would God be so willing to commune to us his personal word, if we have not got the faith or courage to obey what is clearly written in the Bible? I could imagine what it must have been like for Martin Luther, to have read the Bible and understand that not everything he believed or at least was taught, was not from the Bible. In fact, it was too often the opposite. You would have thought that if you show a "believer" what the Bible says, they would change from their religious theology to the truth, but what the Bible says does not seem to matter very much to a high percentage of "believers". Even though they like to think it does. And if you discuss with them that what they preach or teach is unbiblical, they will say, "It's what I said and not what I meant".

If they read the Bible in Mathew 5:37 and 12:36, they would be careful what they say, more importantly say what they mean, and do not talk so lightly. Probably the most effective way of getting bad teaching is to take one isolated verse and try to make it say or mean something that it doesn't (using it out of context). I used to say I could write a book about this subject because there are so many, yet here I am writing the book. We see in the Bible that the devil quoted verses out of context for his own agenda all the time. But Jesus knew better not to be fooled by this as Jesus knew the Bible in its proper context. Therefore, it is a bad problem or even evil to do this and to build whole teachings based on one isolated verse. Yet all this is too common. Many of the wrong traditional thinking came from an isolated Bible verse taken out of context. To quote the Bible out of context is a devil like act, and to quote Bible in context is Christ like. That is why Martin Luther had many things in his complaint in the 95 Theses. The main thing was the Church of Rome had their teachings down on paper to prove their teachings, while many of the teachings in Churchianity are unwritten rules which most Christians obey without question. As long as they do not smoke, drink, or have sexual relations outside of marriage, they think it is all good.

(1) Love God serve man; Love man serve God-----------
---or---------------Luke4:8......you shall worship the Lord your God and him only you shall serve. Plus, Colossians 3:23, Galatians 1:10, Mathew 6:24

(2) You must give a minister a title before his name-----
---or----------Mathew 23:8 But you, do not be called Rabbi.

For one is your teacher, the Christ, and you are all brethren. Do not call anyone on earth your father, for one is your father, he who is in heaven. And do not be called teachers; for one is your teacher the Christ.

(3) We are all children of God, and he is father of us all----------or-------------1 John3:10 In this the children of God and the devil are manifest: Whoever does not practice righteousness is not of God, nor is he who does not love his brother. Also John1:12, Romans 8:9-16, Romans 9-8, Colossians 3:6

(4) We are all guilty before God, Christian and all--------------or---------------2 Corinthians 5:21 God made him who had no sin to be sin for us, so that in him we might become the righteousness of God. Also, 1 Peter 1:19

(5) Come as you are in prayer and/or get worthy enough---------------or ---------------John 14:6, Jesus said to him, "I am the way the truth, and the life. No one comes to the father except through me. Also, John 14:13

(6) Just do your best that's all you can do and try hard to be Christ like------------or ------------ John5:19, Then Jesus answered and said to them, "most assuredly I say to you, the son can do nothing of himself, but what he sees the Father do; for whatever he does, the son does in like manner. Also, Philippians 4:13

(7) You may give up on God, but he will not give up on you-------------------or------------------2 Thessalonians 2:10-

11 ....because they did not receive the love of the truth, that they may be saved. And for this reason, God will send them strong delusion, that they should believe the lie.

(8) God will meet your need and not your greed, (nothing above needed) -----------or-----------------Psalm 37:4, Delight yourself also in the Lord and he will give you the desires of your heart. Also Psalm 20:4, John2:7-9

(9) God answers to religious desperation and need. Just cry hard -----------------or-------------Ephesians 2:8 For by grace you have been saved through faith; and not that of yourselves, it is a gift of God. Also Romans 9:31

(10) God is a gentleman and will not do anything against your free will------------or--------------Romans 9:18 Therefore he has mercy on whom he wills, and whom he wills he hardens. Also Revelation 20:10

(11) In Christ, God cannot see you, he can only see Jesus---------------------or---------------------- Luke12:7 Even the very hairs of your head are all numbered .... Also, Isaiah 49:16

(12) God will turn your tears into prayers, just cry for an answer--------or--------------------Malachi 2:13 And this is the second thing that you do: you cover the altar of the Lord with tears, with weeping and crying; So, he does not regard the offering anymore, nor receive it with goodwill from your hands. Also, Mark 5:38-40

(13) All that matters is that you pray from the heart, that's all we can do-----------or -------------------Ephesians 6:18 Praying always with all prayer and supplication in the Spirit............ Also, Hebrews 11:6

(14) Give God your best and then he will give you his best -----------------or--------------------Romans 5:8 But God demonstrates his love toward us, in that, while we were still sinners, Christ died for us.

(15) Much prayer much blessing, little prayer little blessing---------------------or--------------------Mathew 6:5-7 And when you pray, do not use vain repetitions as the heathen do. For they think that they will be heard for their many words.

(16) We must be sensitive to people's feelings when prayer in church-----------or----------------- Galatians 1:10 For do I now persuade men, or God? Or do I seek to please men? For if I yet pleased men, I should not be a servant of Christ.

(17) There is no right or wrong way to pray, just do your best-----------------or------------------- Jude 1:20 But you, beloved, building yourselves up on your most holy faith, praying in the Holy Spirit, Also Romans 8:26 Ephesians 6:18, John 4:24

(18) Obey your leaders mainly spiritual in all things, no questions----------------or ------------------1 Peter 5:3 Nor as

being Lords over those entrusted to you, but being examples to the flock. Also, Galatians 1:8

(19) God cannot get close to sin. --------------------or----- ------------------ Luke 22:47 .... And he who was called Judas, one of the twelve, went before them and drew near to Jesus to kiss him. Also, Luke 7:38

(20) God could not look at Jesus on the cross as it was too hard for him--------------or--------------------Isaiah 53:10 But the Lord was pleased to crush him and to cause him to suffer; .... Also, 2 Corinthians 9:7

I could go on and on, as too often I hear "believers" say things about God and how to pray. That is not biblical advice but popular opinions. These days especially on social media, they appear to be painting a picture of who they think God is according to a projection of themselves, who their identity is in, and who they think they are before God based on popular opinion. Almost every other day I read on social media and hear from Church folks, quotes that they think are Biblical, yet are so ignorant and wrong. I sometimes wonder have they even read the Bible, at all? Some Churches appear to have so many extremes which go from one to the other with pride appearing to be a major factor. I recently read an article lately, saying that the Church is married to poverty, prisons, and hardships. The same people were giving harsh words to the other believers in the extreme teaching of prosperity. Talk about throwing the baby out with the bath water, and the pot calling the kettle black. This is so bad that I used to wonder am I the only person to have read the Bible, just like that sign at the rock concert many years ago that said – the 'way in'. Yes, we have hard times and can be put in prison, but we are not married to them. Our covenant is in Christ. I do believe that others have read the Bible, but it seems to have as much significance to them as popular spiritual junk. I recall thinking that some Church folks will believe anything but the Bible, as long as the quote has some religious tone to it. They will accept it as their gospel, yet the Bible verses goes over them like water off a duck's back. I hear statements often of faith like, 'God will never let us go through more than we can handle'! Yet I read in the Bible from Paul in 2 Corinthians 1:8-9

"For we would not, brethren have you ignorant of our trouble which came to us in Asia, that we were pressed out of measure, above strength, insomuch that we despaired even of life. Yes, we had the sentence of death in ourselves that we should not trust in ourselves but in God who raises the dead".

It's too often I hear statements of faith not only without folk question them, but they are popular statements, so popular that they come across as bible verses. But if I even dare to bring these quotes to fellow believers and show that they are very unbiblical, I would get a funny look and be left alone. Christianity gets its beliefs from the Bible,

52

Churchianity gets its beliefs from the pulpit and popular opinions. Wrong beliefs affect how we see God and ourselves, this in turn will affect our communication (prayer) with God. To pray right we must believe right. No wonder the prayer lives and meetings are repetitive, powerless, empty, and such an approachable thing to "believers".

They do not smoke, drink, smile, and have morals. But if you ask them if they have love for themselves, the answer would most likely be a high percentage of no. I know this as I asked many times to myself. Additionally, their prayer life appears to be dead, traditional, and superstitious. However, they do not worry about that as it is their normal and popular in their Church. This upsets me and has done for so many years. The thing is, I know I am not a very good Christian, yet I know the difference and know better. If you try talking to an ignorant person and ask a simple question (that will show their ignorance), they will ignore the question and put words into your mouth that you did not say. Then try to change the subject. Once this happens, just stop arguing, and move on.

As I have said, we all have different strengths, weaknesses, and blind spots. My weakness seemed to be in connection with people. I loved to get people's attention, but never wanted to give them mine. I could tell them about myself, but I was never concerned about them. The most self-centred, self-critical, unthankful person I knew was myself. Deep inside it appeared to be a self-hate and feeling of not worthy of love from such a young age, it was my normal. My life was totally taken over with striving for acceptance, yet without being their clone. Yes, I was looking for inner peace and something. After I become a Christian in one way, I found what I was looking for. But I did not have much peace and I did not know what love was. I had no problem knowing God would put me in hell if I was not saved, but the love of God felt alien to me. So, I had faith to get saved, but no faith to get love. My insecurity started to get out of control, and it destroyed parts of my life and relationships with almost everyone, earlier in my faith. A few things did help me. Knowing that as a Christian, condemnation is from the devil to bring me down and is wrong. Also, conviction that may humble me a moment to repent, then lifts me is from God. I read teaching on life and death is in the power of the tongue and soon realised I was my own worst enemy in that part. My own prayer life was very repetitive. It was all about my best efforts. In Church prayer meetings, it was the same few people praying the same prayers week in and week out, year in and year out. It was and sadly still, is very predictable. The Catholic chapel have a prayer for this and a prayer for that. Saying prayers, but not in communion with God in prayer. Likewise, the church seems to have prayers for this and that, yet with next to no communication with God. One thing that will help bring fast changes to a prayer life is prayer with fasting. It seems to clear the ways more with a more powerful connection experience of the Lord. But fasting is only mentioned a few times in New Testament, yet warning us what teachings not to believe is very popular. I have had to change what I believe many times as a Christian as I grew more in truth. The truth will set us free, but from what!? A lie that we have already believed at several times. But are there many people who really are willing to question or check what they already think is the truth!!? That will take true humility and courage.

On the day of my salvation when men prayed for me, their countenance changed, and things happened. During communion at Church when a man prayed, I could immediately tell he had been with Jesus in prayer. Prayer seemed to be something that was very important in the Bible, but no matter how hard I tried, it did not seem to be going right and it felt like playing a record constantly. I go to highly respected believers and they tell me it just takes time. More time and more trying. With the same dedication as I put into becoming a champion sports man, I put the same effort into praying, yet I was only left frustrated and disappointed. One day walking home from Church, I remember saying to God that "I know fully that I have been giving prayer my best efforts for two years and I still cannot get it right". I told God that, "I cannot pray, and I do not know how". Instantly I heard a word from God in my heart "now you can". The pride of "I can do it with self-effort" was broken. I wasn't too sure what this meant at the time. But what I do know is, the next time I prayed was different. It felt like I was connecting more with God. Then I remembered a prayer experience I had when I first became a Christian. I completed a week of Christian youth work and about six months after I became a Christian. I remember when I went to pray, it was totally different. My prayer now sounded more like the prayers in the Bible, both the Psalms and the New Testament. I was like a spectator to my own praying to an extent, and I was listening to it myself. I was not sure what it was and never heard of it in a Church. I had been to many prayer meetings in Churches and heard highly respected men of God pray, but I never heard this. I did not know what it was. Sadly, this should have been the most common thing in Church, however I never heard of it. It was the Holy Spirit helping me flow in prayer precisely. The only thing I was asked that I felt within my heart from God, was not to have my own agenda at times when praying. That week I was seeing great things happen and the leaders could tell that God was with me. After that week I remember getting a word from God, that in the future this kind of praying will be my new normal. In the past I was so fearful of public prayer, that I asked the Pastors never to ask me to pray publicly as I was so terrified of that thought. But after my second year as a

Christian when I started to pray in the prayer meetings, some people began to feel connected to GOD and felt uplifted. After my second time praying at a prayer meeting, people clapped in applause. It felt good when older ladies were approaching me to tell me that my praying encouraged them. A few people may have thought it was just a short faze but week after week my praying became more effective, unpredictable, and fresh. Some Church leaders who used to pray their best, using professional repetitive stuff, stopped praying. What used to seem to be the real deal was shown for what it was, soulish performance praying. They felt uncomfortable with me there. It was obvious God had done something, but the Church really never showed interest as it was outside of their domain of understanding as was I. After all I did not wear a shirt, tie, and suit like them. So, how could God be with me? lol. A few occasions during fasting and praying, It felt really powerful, but just like an old habit over time. The old ways and good intentions of praying would come back. I would try to manipulate God in prayer by telling him what I thought he wanted to hear with thanks and praise then tell him what I really wanted and put "in Jesus' name" at the end of the prayer to try to make it official. But that is how I used to pray before I was a Christian. It is how you pray in Churchianity. I call them the "would you prayers". Like chatting with a girl in a pub, you tell her what you think she wants to hear, in order to take from her what you want. Sadly, people think that is how God is. They get a verse from the Bible about coming to God with thanks and praise, to tell God what you think he wants to hear thinking that will build up your chances of getting from him what you want. Gratitude and praise in itself is good, but it does not earn us some kind of grace, and it does not change God's mind about us. Gratitude and praise are to help our minds about who God is. It is not to change his mind about us.

After nearly 25 years as a Christian, I can sadly say that prayer meetings have been needlessly repetitive and joyless, with numbers getting smaller. I have been to many prayer meetings in different towns and when I turned up to some of them, there was only myself there unless someone else had to come to open the doors. It is an embarrassment. Then I went to most of the others and it was the same. "Would you" prayer after "would you" pray, the same old traditional ways? Just like king Saul saw young David's God given success as a threat to him. The cold shoulder treatment was pretty normal to me. Then as the years and decades gone by, I noticed that there was plenty of doom, gloom, and tears in the prayers over and over again, prayer after a prayer. Yet I was gloomy for years in Churchianity, but with God's help he got me out of such beliefs, and the result was when I went into a prayer meeting, I was again totally different and very joyful. I could not understand this. It was the normal for others to be begging, pleading God and crying, trying to get God's attention to do something. Praying as if God was a cold-hearted person who took a lot of convincing to care to do something. Then I would pray at a completely different wave length or should I say a different spirit with joy and gladness. Then after my prayer with God it would be silence, as they just didn't know what to do or how to react after it, as my prayers seemed to be an interruption to their religious duties. After a while, someone would lift up the doom and gloom baton and carry it on. I used to wonder was I being wrong or ignorant. I asked God, "is there something wrong with me, as I am very joyful in prayer meetings at Church, and yet a high percentage of "believers" showed doom, gloom and lots of tears". After praying about this, an idea popped up to me to look up in the Old Testament, where it talks about the house of prayer and what God would do for people that honoured him. In holding fast his covenant in the previous verses, this is what GOD said he would do to them - Isaiah 56:7

"Even them I will bring to my holy mountain, and make them joyful in my house of prayer. Their burnt offerings and their sacrifices will be accepted on my alter; For my house shall be called a house of prayer for all nations".

According to the Bible, God makes those- joyful in the house of prayer, who honour his covenant. You would think that most "believers" would read this and have an honest analysis at how they pray and then make changes, but to the ninety-nine percent, the evidence or the clear truth does not matter and is not enough to them. It seems like the Bible does not matter to them, as they refuse to let the Bible interfere with their religious beliefs and traditional ways. And they are in denial of what is outside of their ignorant box. What the Bible says does not mean much to them, although they think it does, but it doesn't; as long as it does not differ from their religious beliefs that they hold onto. All that seems to matter to them is playing some kind of religious game where the Preacher wants to please the people, and the people want to please the Preacher. Ticking each other's boxes and fulfilling each other's expectations. I attended many Churches and told believers about my experience in prayer meetings. Sharing what the Bible says, but just like the WAY IN sign was in clear black and white then did not matter. The clear truth just did not matter much now either. The sin of denial.

Again, I asked God why people cry, beg, and plead so much during prayer meetings. I felt that it is because they are trying to earn and atone in prayer to get an answer. No faith in Jesus' name and what Jesus did on the cross was enough for them. They feel they have to have some suffering during their prayers to make it count and pay credit to getting the answer. I remember myself like this with years of crying daily, many long hours of "praying" and yet no results to show for it. It is called tears of unbelief, or wrong belief. Many times, from the pulpit it is taught that God turns our tears into prayers answered. This comes from a verse in the Bible where God said "I have seen your tears" however, God did not say we just have to cry sadly in need, and I will turn your tears into prayers, a very bad conclusion. Yes, many times the Bible talks about folks crying out to God, but that was more a call from the heart. To think that God answered because they were simply crying is unreasonable. Tears, begging, pleading, long prayers, and even the giving of gratitude, praise, and worship does not get us credit before God, or earn anything with him. There appears to be great misunderstanding about tears and crying in prayer. Another Bible verse says that 'God is close to the broken hearted'. So sadly, again the wrong conclusion is drawn that believers will get God to draw closer because they are playing a victim, and then to think they have a better chance to be heard with God if they are broken hearted! This is called dead works, to think you can earn God's grace by being broken and sad. It is our true faith where the LORD JESUS CHRIST is and what he did on the cross for us, and knowing who we are to him and accepted by the beloved. All thanksgiving, praise, and worship is not to be accepted by God or earns his favour, it is because according to Christ we already are. It does seem very difficult for Christians to believe in the Bible over ignorant tradition.

Chapter 11

What does it mean to pray in Jesus' name?

To pray in Jesus' name, does not mean to stick his name on the end of your soulish prayer to try and justify it, and fool other people that it is rightly done. Praying in Jesus' name means coming to God believing in Christ and his righteousness, and read the Bible. Both Peter and Paul raised the dead and did not mention the name of Jesus at the end of their prayer, yet a thousand "believers" can pray the ignorant way in Jesus's name, and not even see a person healed of a common cold. One way is Biblical, and it works. The other popular way is Churchianity, but this does not work. What way does most believers choose to pray? Sometimes, I do mention Jesus' name at the end of prayer, but hopefully not out of superstition to be just stuck at the end of the prayer to perform well. Truth be told, that if I mention Jesus' name at the end of the prayer, it now makes me question myself, did I really pray as it means in Jesus' name?

Mathew 7:22, talks about what Jesus will do to people who think they are serving him because they do it "in his name". Religion and even praying in Jesus's name can be wrong. It is so easy to tell the difference, just read the Bible and have the courage to be honest with it. The mouth will say "Lord have your way" but the heart will say "as long as it is our old way".

Many times in prayer meetings, the thing that I was led to pray was the very verses and subjects the minister was teaching on. I was the odd one pointed out for this. I just seemed to make others feel uncomfortable that God would accept or use me as I don't tick their boxes.

Chapter 12

Identity crisis that Churchianity makes worse. Where insecurities grow.

I remember before I was a Christian, I would feel very uncomfortable if a man with a better body than me was near me, and felt insecure. I would see a great shaped man as a threat to my identity, instead of being happy for him, want to complement him, and learn from him. Sadly, that also is too common among Christians when others with more talent, gifting, or anything that comes near them, they feel insecure. Even a believer with little money or success in an area of life, will be tempted to hate a person out of jealousy who has a bigger level of success and money. We belong in the same family of God and should always want the best for each other. Someone who is more talented or gifted can and will be seen as a threat. A foreign Preacher I knew (with high levels of success), was stopped by religious leaders in Northern Ireland because he was seen as evil, as he did things that local preachers only talked about. Denial and insecurity are the first results of the fall of man. Adam and Eve illustrated this, yet these subjects are rarely talked about. The priority appears to be - do not smoke, drink, take drugs, or have sexual immorality; but they rarely seem to get to the root issues. Adam and Eve was not smoking, drinking, doing drugs, or any sexual immorality first thing as the result of the fall, but it was the first denial before God, and they were very insecure. They lost their peace with God, themselves, and each other; as they started to see themselves as unworthy of God's love, which made them lose peace with each other. They had seen themselves as unacceptable.

2 Corinthians 5:21

"For he made him who knew no sin to be sin on our behalf, so that we might become the righteousness of God in him."

This is the good news, the gospel. Our identity as Christians is in Christ, and not in works. This is a fundamental belief in the Christian faith but sadly, many believers appear to not to be with the Christian faith, because they believe in Churchianity. They may like to say they believe the Bible, but will quote "we are all still unworthy, dirty sinners, lowly beggars" and many more. However, if you tell believers they are who the Bible says they are, some will get angry or sometimes will try to believe both. You cannot truly believe simultaneously two different things if they contradict each other. Having this wrong view of who they are, how they see themselves before God, and how they see God; will affect how they pray along with everything else. The religious junk will not only cause spiritual constipation, but the religious junk is what needs to be pooped out in the first place. That is why I feel that after twenty odd years as a Christian, a very high percentage of the Church are still praying the same prayers day in and day out, decade in and decade out, with prayer meetings getting smaller in numbers; instead of going from faith to faith and glory to glory.

Chapter 13

If God says you got something, the religious demons says you do not.

It can be challenging to lead properly in a prayer meeting. Some can have little trust in how the congregation will pray, that they do not let them pray during the prayer meetings; and when they let a few people pray, they almost always pray to God to do what he has already done. It is as ignorant as praying for fire to be hot and ice to be cold. Like a dog chasing its own tail trying to get what it already has, likewise believers pray to God to send his spirit, to give them authority, to be with them, and to be with other believers. This is the total opposite of the Bible verse Philemon1:6.

"That the sharing of your faith may become effective by the acknowledgment of every good thing which is in you in Christ Jesus."

We find out here that there is effectiveness in acknowledging the good we have in Christ, yet the opposite of that is talking or praying as though we are not in the goodness of Christ, instead of praying who we are in Christ and declaring all that God has already done. Most seem to be asking God to do the thing he already does and promised. Why do not people believe God for a change? IF God says we have something in us already, then we have it, and should stop looking and asking for it. When God says we have something, and a religious demon says we don't, how many

67

folks believe? Religious ignorance keeps asking God to do what he already does and seeks for what we already have. I am sure you would agree that evil will either do something that looks like the truth or do something that is the opposite of truth. For example, if God said go north then evil will go south. If God said something is black, evil will say it is white.

When God said do not eat from one tree, what did they do? Well, as you know it was not smoking or drinking that was the problem, it was doing the opposite of the word of God, and eating from that one tree. But again, the Bible gives us an example of faith in how at times it works in calling things that are not as though they were.

In Romans 4:17 (as it is written, "I have made you a father of many nations") in the presence of him whom he believed – God, who gives life to the dead and calls those things which are not as though they were". And the opposite of that is to call things that are as though they are not. We are blessed with the faith in Christ and the Lord is always with us not to leave us or forsake us yet. A high percentage of praying in Churches is asking God to bless who he said he already blessed, then they ask God to be with whom he already said he was with. For example praying "Please Lord send your spirit when he already has, give us authority over evil, that he already has, and the list goes on and on.

I recall a good minister who purposely set up a test on social media illustrating unbiblical religious quotes, with almost everyone not knowing the difference. After his calculations, he found out that ninety seven percent of Christians did not know the difference, or that he was wrong. Ignorance and being blind to the full truth affect firstly, what believers see and how they pray. Secondly, when ignorance is common and accepted, when the truth comes out, they think it is wrong. Just as the ignorance in people who hated Jesus two thousand years ago, that they will not want a person of truth now or ever. Then another problem is denial. A person in denial has the knowledge but does not have the courage to do anything about it. Because of the fear of man, there is pressure from the Church towards the minister to pray in a way that will please them in the way they expect.

Then there is also pressure from the minister to the church to pray in a way that pleases him and what he expects. Ticking each other's boxes is playing religious games. If a minister was to pray and not mention some of the sick who were not there to be healed, then someone in the church will remember for one week what he did for others. In their ignorant insecurity, they will be offended and will complain. Believers try too hard to please God but, the sad thing is they want to please man on an equal basis. My own weakness at times is to please myself more than God. But the BBible says we cannot serve two masters,

Mathew 6:24.

"I asked God why believers do that, and I got the answer. They try to serve God and man on an equal basis."

A few days later, I noticed religious folks of Churchianity had posted their own man-made quotes on their Church page saying –Love God and serve man, and love man and serve God. Just as the Lord told me what they believe, seeing their quote confirmed the word I got. As I read their quote,

God told me "I never said that, I said" Luke 4:8 "you shall worship the Lord your God, and him only you shall serve."

When the Lord Jesus was teaching about praying, he not only taught how to pray, but he gave examples on how not to pray also, and in doing so, many would have been offended as Jesus even repeated how they prayed through examples. However, in Churches some truths are told about how to pray, but very little is ever spoken about how not to pray. Even when a minister knows clearly when prayer is wrong, he will not dare to challenge or rebuke the person much, unless it is a different kind of ignorance to what they have accepted.

Sadly, when believers try to point out a wrong, they come across so vague and sensitive that the communication is not clear enough to get to the point. If we want to pray as Christians, Christ- like, then we need to be taught Christ like. Can I be taught by a football coach to get the results of a boxing coach? Can I be taught with a driving instructor to achieve the results of a dart player? If I want proper boxing lessons, I would need to go to a boxing coach and so on. If the Church wants to pray Christ- like, they will need to be taught Christ- like. Jesus said he can do nothing unless the Father shows him first. When I pray, I get tuned into him more clearly from a time of praise and worship; and during this time, at times I wait on our father to show me what he wants me to pray. I know there will be at times an overflow of joyful praise during these times, while other times I just have an idea but I rejoice in that. I do not know what or how the prayer will go, which in turn leaves me in a vulnerable place in which I have no choice but to trust God. The more that happens, the more powerful the prayer is, and I have to give glory to God knowing it was guided by his Holy Spirit. Our prayer to God is vital, and what we believe can and will have a big effect in that, either for good or bad. During these days where there is lock down and we can't meet with fellow believers often, our personal prayer life is much more important.

I recall having a vision for many years, of me being a banana on what I thought was an apple tree, surrounded with apples and I was the odd one out who was not wanted. I was the ugly duckling. A few years ago, I became a Christian after eighteen years, I received a word from God that I was not a banana on that apple tree, but I was a banana on a banana tree that was surrounded with apples hanging on it. Illegitimate fruit hanging on it like Christmas decorations. That weekend a person spoke about false fruits, just what I was shown, which confirmed the word I got from God.

After many years of either being the odd one in a prayer meeting or the only one in attendance, I heard that there was a large gathering of Christians from different Churches to have a prayer meeting. I said to myself that this will be interesting as each Church knows what "prayers" to pray, what is expected of them, and what will be pleasing to the others in their local church etc. Just as Catholics know what prayers to pray along with, so does each denomination of the religion of Churchianity know what "prayers" to pray. Now as they were mixed with different denominations together, I wondered what they would do, or how could they pray or cope without their religious measures to know what is right or accepted. To be honest, I was not expecting anyone to pray as I knew they were outside of their comfort zone and do not know what "prayers" to pray. The minister said a few words, then left the floor open for people to start praying. There were hundreds of "believers" present, but the room was quiet. I waited for a long time and kept on waiting. I felt very embarrassed for fellow Christians there, along with other Church denominations who continued to watch and wait as nothing happened. After waiting on others to pray for far too long, I became frustrated, I stood up, and began to pray for the people in the room in the hope that this would awaken them from their spiritual sleep. So, with loads of fire in my belly, I continued to pray, and I included a few Bible verses that come to me. Then that was it. Only myself prayed that day while the other 99% were too bounded up with Churchianity to do any better. Hundreds of men were in attendance, but it felt that they had lost their masculinity and courage to pray as men. They may not smoke, or drink, and have morals, but where is the love for the Lord in prayer? The minister who stood up at the end to finish the meeting to speak on a Bible verse which, was the same one as I prayed about. However, he did acknowledge me for saying it. It feels that all what really matters to Churchianity is that you do not smoke or drink publicly, have good morals, wear a shirt and tie, and do not be too manly. The big problem is not the lack of Bible verses, as much as believing religious lies that are taken as Biblical doctrine, in Mathew 6:6 when Jesus warned about this.

If there were two men standing together and one of them had a healthy eating lifestyle and went to the gym often while the other was unhealthy in his diet and fitness, would you think you could tell the difference easily by looking at them? Of course you would. Likewise, Jesus said it is by their fruit that you will know them. Likewise, we can tell a lot about a person when they pray.

I could go on about "praying" that people declaring who was not going to be healed, who was not going to get saved, who will go to hell, and even prayers for God to "remove" people. Even some prayers reflect that the devil is big and God is small. To pray properly as a Christian, people will need to believe properly. If we believe what the Christians believed in the Bible, then we will pray as they did too. When we talk about the reading of Paul's prayers, he has a similar way throughout his books. Yet, it is almost unheard of, as the traditional way is different. Does our prayers show that we believe in God and his word? Or does things like feelings, fears, unbelief, and tradition get in the way too much? As how we pray will affect how we live.

However, there is hope as I know I used to be the most cowardly person about prayer, with not much faith in God. I would go as far to say that my prayers were doing more damage than good. If God can change how, I see prayer as he desires, then he can do it to whosoever is truly wanting to learn correctly. Many times, my prayer is very passionate, joyful, and pleasurable which is available to all in Christ.

Psalm 16:11... "In the presence of the Lord is fullness of joy; at your right hand are pleasures forevermore."

This is what the Bible teaches, but Churchianity says it is mostly doom and gloom, and prayer is a time to be depressed about hardships. Yes, of course there is a time to weep with those who weep, but decades passed by and most people praying appears to be quite gloomy, joyless, and powerless with little hope. What way of praying do you believe in? Do not deceive yourself if you think you believe the Bible yet follow Churchianity, and their "dear Jesus" that is according to their own religious ideas and culture. The truth seems to be hitting hard and quite harsh at times. Still to this day, at times my life's prayers can seem dry, usually it's some repetitiveness, unbelief, or wrong belief that has crept in slowly. Times like these, it is good to be still and wait on the Lord. Just as there can be a temptation to try to impress and put on some performance in public prayer, even in our private time we can have a temptation to try to impress God with our performance in prayer without even showing it off. We can please God by faith, but that is stupid pride to think we can impress God with our best performances in "prayer". Just as some people think praying in old English, will please God.

One night as I was looking through my Bible, I stumbled upon the same chapter that Jesus had quoted saying "My house shall be called a house of prayer for all nations". As I read a few verses later, about God giving a word to his spiritual leaders, from Isaiah 56:10 which read

"His watchmen are blind, they are all ignorant; they are all dumb dogs, they cannot bark; Sleeping, lying down, loving to slumber."

Wow, I perceive them as some harsh words from God. The God of the BBible and not a blue eyed soft feminine God from Churchianity. The Lord made it clear to me as the Lord tells us in Mathew 26:41,

"Watch and pray... Both watch and pray and not just one or the other."

Jesus could do nothing only what the father showed him, which means total dependence on the Lord to do so. Then, by the Holy Spirit we can watch and pray. However, if the heart has hardened to the word of God, and the eyes blinded with religion; then his watch men (God's people) will be blind. They will remain in their ignorance, close to what I have talked about. They will be dumb (spiritually dumb) and will not be able to bark (make the sound that is needed - say or pray as needed) and will be sleeping, (spiritually sleeping). People need to stop following religion and believing everything a person says, even though that person has been right in many other things. In following the Lord Jesus Christ's example in prayer, we will know what it is to meet with God our Father.

Chapter 14
The difference between the men of God and the false religious praying in the Bible.

When we read of how Joshua prayed, it stated that he loved to spend time with God. Then, when it comes to needing a miracle, Joshua 10:1-15. God told Joshua to tell the sun to stand still and it did. No begging and crying, no going on and on in prayer, hoping to try and twist God's arms to do something, and no telling God what to do. God told Joshua what to do and he spoke to the sun to stand still and it did. The prayer of faith speaks to the problem. Prayer is mostly about meeting with God our father and when needed, we hear from God what to do and we do it or speak the prayer of faith to resolve a problem. The same thing with Elijah, he of course knew how to pray. Then there were the rebellious people of God who left God and ran after false religion (sounds familiar). When it comes time to seeing who is right between the two, Elijah asked them to pray to whom they thought God was and he will pray to whom the true God is, with proper prayer of course in truth. The challenge was to see who saw the display of the power of God to answer. We read this in 1 Kings 18. The ways of ignorant people were in their praying as they kept begging and pleading the God of their deception, with no answer. They continued to beg and plead more, and cry very hard with much desperation; then because emotional atonement was not enough, they began cutting themselves. After all, they believe that their suffering in prayer with many tears was going to twist their god's arm and hopefully receive an answer, yet with no answer. Sounds familiar. Elijah was mocking them in their ignorance. There way was popular, cultural, and traditional, which their spiritual leaders had taught them this way. Yet, still nothing happened. Then came Elijah's turn, a person of truth who really knew God. He just prayed a few words, and with fire coming down, God answered him. Who does your local church sound like in prayer? Who do you sound like? Elijah or the false religion?

Chapter 15
Praying as a New Covenant believer.

When it comes to the new covenant, time and time again, when it came to a miracle of healing, it was just a short prayer of faith speaking in authority to the situation. Never did the apostles say to the sick that they would say prayers for them in a prayer meeting to tell God to heal them. Yet, today how will "believers" react if they see a person in need of healing who wants prayer for healing? Would they lay on hands and pray "in the name of Jesus Christ be healed" (the biblical Christian way)? Or would they tell the sick that they will wait until a prayer meeting to tell God what to do about it, (the traditional Churchianity way)?

Prayer, first and foremost, is to meet with God and not just to try to get something. God is not a stepping stone that we stand on to help us reach for something higher and more critical. How can a person claim or believe to be talking to almighty God without having awe and excitement? I know that if I was to pray and my motives were wrong and my heart not in it, all it takes is for me to be honest with God about it and say sorry or repent. God, in His grace, seems to honour my honesty, and he changes how the prayer goes. Now, the thought of praying makes me excited at times. Never one time has the Spirit of God led me to pray in a way that resembles anything like Churchianity, and it is always according to his word with life and energy as it goes. People sadly think if something sounds like the truth then, it must be the truth.

Chapter 16

The fake will try to copy the real. And greater punishment if you should have known better.

Some who have read the Bible can easily see fault in a prayer of a person who has not, and think that they are okay as they sound much correct. But sounding more correct does not make it okay, as a fake £20 note that looks better than another fake £20 note, does not make that okay. After knowing the Bible, we should be more careful to heed it in our life, as well as the prayer. The Bible says in Luke 12: 46-48:

"The master of the servant will come in a day when he is not looking for him, and at an hour when he is not aware, and will cut him in two and appoint him his portion with the unbelievers. That servant who knew his master's will and did not prepare himself or do according to his will, shall be beaten with many stripes. But he who did not know, yet committed things deserving of stripes, shall be beaten with few. For everyone to whom much is given, from him much will be required; and to whom much has been committed, of them they will ask the more."

Chapter 17
God answers faith and not a victim mentality.

Another misbelief about God and prayer, is to believe the needier we are, then we have more chance of God giving us our need. This comes from the teaching I previously mentioned before that "God will meet our need and not our greed". Giving the wrong conclusion that unless you really need something then God won't give it, and if you are in real desperation then you have got a better chance of getting an answer. Yes, the Bible does say God will meet our needs, however, the way many have perceived that for years, mixed with false humility quotes, has made believers think the best chance to get an answer from God; is to be totally desperate and very needy to the point of crying in tears with pleading and begging. Yet these mindsets and ignorant beliefs think if they pretend they have nothing then they will get something from God. Yet the Bible says, Mathew 13:12

"For whoever has, more shall be given, and he will have abundance; but whoever does not have, even what he has will be taken away from him".

Like I said before from the Bible, there is power and results from acknowledging the good, we have in our Christ. Not in acting as a victim. When we think of the first miracle Jesus performed in the Bible, it was not to heal the sick or give supernatural abundance to the poor but rather, it was to turn water into wine. These people had already plenty and used it all. Mary had faith in Jesus to provide, and we know the rest of the story of Jesus turning the water into wine. That was not a need, it was their heart's desire and with faith they got it. Yet, the many people who were suffering did not get anything from the Lord. A better conclusion is that God answers faith in him. As he is a merciful AND a generous God, with much more than just being in need. When the disciples went fishing with the Lord's blessing, they gained much more abundance. When the Lord fed the thousands of people, there was abundance more than they could eat with plenty left over. God loved us so much, that he gave us his son. God is not tight fisted.

Our Lord Jesus Christ paid for us to be blessed in him. We cannot pay for our blessings by being sad, desperate, and needy in prayer. I spent many years praying like this, trying to make God pity me and want to bless me. Praying my tears of unbelief and always living a life as an orphan, feeling like I was totally overlooked and forgotten about, or feeling at least I must not have mattered much to God as my life was so miserable. Playing the victim and some self-pity NEVER got me answers to prayer or helped. However, as long as I did not smoke, drink, and had some morals, the Church was happy; and of course put the money in the box. Now, daily at times by the grace of God I am rejoicing greatly in the Lord and now know how blessed I am by the Lord, to have him with me (the almighty God) and to sense him with me or hear his word. Such excitement at times I feel about mostly what is to come, more blessings and provision flowing to me without striving for it. Most of my prayer is a strong desire just to worship God for the joy of it and the pleasure in just being with God. It really is a wonderful thing. Remember according to the Bible, these are pleasing to God's covenant, he will make them joyful in the house of prayer. However, Churchianity does not believe in that, rather it believes in self-oppression, suffering, crying, begging, and pleading will earn God's grace to answer or at least make him have to answer out of pity and popular pressure. Yet the only time we read of a group of people praying anything like Churchianity, was when they were praying long prayers through the night for Peter's release. Yet when Peter was knocking on the door they did not believe. When Peter spoke, they still did not believe, even after hearing his voice. Therefore, that long prayer meeting was more of a show of unbelief, yet too many folks take this prayer meeting of unbelief as an example of how to pray.

Thankfully, our life is not in the hands of people's lack of faith, but in God. Yet this one event of people with very little faith or any at all is taken as the example, of how to pray in a Church when hard times are present. This appears too common within Church, to get a few verses that happen to one group or one event in the Bible, and they think this is the common way to live or pray. At the same time, get what is very popular in the Bible and treat it as if it is not even heard of. In other words, they follow the exception rather than the rule. When both Marys came to Jesus' crying, and in much pain, need and desperation over their dead brother Lazarus, did he say he will turn their tears into prayers!? Of course not! He said, John 11:40 Jesus said to her,

"Did I not say to you that if you would believe you would see the glory of God?"

Again, we see it's not begging and pleading God, but rather belief in God that gets answers. We also read in Joshua1:8 that Joshua meditated on the word of God to live it and he will make his way prosperous. As we can see again, this looks nothing like the orphan's begging. To pray is not a burden we must endure, to tick a box to keep in God's good books, and/or keep him happy. But it is our greatest blessing, joy, honour, and privilege we can ever have. I hope people realise that Christianity prayer is better than Churchianity prayers. God will not hold us to a standard that is based on what a Church has said is important, but according to his words. That is how we are to go to God in prayer, not according to what is popular in a Church, but according to his word. If we pray according to the word of God, then we will be in direct contact with God, much more easily, and hear from God better.

As I learned to pray as the Bible teaches, I then started to sound by the Holy Spirit as they did in the Bible, and I experienced God closer to me. Just like when I believed as they did, I prayed in the flesh (good intentions) as they did. God would seem distant and I sounded in prayer nothing like they do in the Bible. But just as the way into the concert, I was available for everyone who purchased a ticket; similarly, to pray as Christians did in the Bible in the Holy Spirit, with joy unspeakable and full of glory, eyes to see what the father is showing, and ears to hear his word, is for everyone in Christ. Of course if you are not a Christian, then you can always ask the Lord to forgive and save you. Because people believe what they want to believe, to make life as easy with others as possible, the temptation will be to want to continue in ignorance because of the cost and uncomfortable changes it can bring to their life. However, just as I stopped and looked around me on that concert day, I was with myself and went the only proper way. We should stop and realise we will have to stand before God and give an account, and knowing the Churchianity excuses will not get us off the hook. If someone gets back more of the fear of God to follow him, there would be a change in how most of Christians live and pray. Just like at the concert, the 99% people had a change in direction and went the same way I was on by myself. Likewise, Church folk would leave their Churchianity, religious, ticking men's boxes, soulless, repeating, predictable, dead, praying within empty prayer meetings to a change of direction. To walk in the true light of the Lord. Not what man says is true, but what the Bible says is true. Then the prayer meetings would be highly attended, powerful, joyful, and hearing from God more clearly. Psalm 34:8

"O Taste and see that the Lord is good; blessed is the man who trust in him."

Chapter 18
Ticking all boxes yet all wrong

A few years ago, I was at a gym changing and I noticed that the floor was quite dirty under the seats, it looked like a build - up of dirt that had accumulated over a long period of time. I informed the manager about this, but she said it was not dirty. I told her in detail how dirty it was, but she insisted that it was clean because she had checked her paperwork, and everyone had ticked the boxes in the cleaning rota. I told her "you may have ticked all the boxes, but it is not done right. In fact I would not have let a dog go there". She still did not believe me, even after I asked her to come and see for herself, but she refused to look. I then took a recording of the mess and sent it to the owner of the gym. He saw it and was shocked. He politely thanked me for the recording and said sorry for the mess in the changing room. It is safe to say the changing room has been clean even years later.

Sadly, some folks are like this, mainly in prayer because of the lack of fear of God. You try to tell them about their Churchianity beliefs and praying, but they seem to be only concerned with ticking all the Churchianity boxes. Try getting them to look at the word is like trying to get the gym manager to look at the floor, they do not want to know. However, unlike the owner of the gym to whom I had to send a recording of the room for him to see. God sees the prayer meetings that are ticking boxes, but to be frank are a mess to what it should be. An ignorant person will ask now, if it is like this then why doesn't God say something? The answer is, I heard God many times rebuke his people about their praying from the gifts of the Holy Spirit, yet after the word is given, folks go back to how they prayed before as if nothing was said. It seems God has spoken, and written word has had no effect on some folk at all. I remember being told a little about how the Bible teaches on how to pray and not to pray, it had an immediate effect to the changes needed. But also, at times God spoke into my life about personal things and I ignored it for many years. I lost out for years because of this reason. Only to hear his word over the subject once again many years later, and after I obeyed the word did I get an answer to a specific prayer. God doesn't have to repeat himself over and over to prove he means what he says.

Chapter 19
The teaching of dying to self.

I have heard it many times in Church about dying to self, even many say it is the main part of their faith. It sounded so religious that I believed it myself for a while, until I began to read the Bible more. I will try make this short as I could write a short book on this subject. Jesus did say to deny ourselves and pick up our cross and daily. That would be not to trust in ourselves, our efforts, and works for salvation. We deny ourselves and put our faith in Jesus for salvation. And then we can trust in the truth that we have been crucified with Christ. The cross was never a reminder of something that happens daily, but of something that was done once and for all the events with Christ. A misunderstanding that helped start the die to self-teaching was from one verse that Paul said "I die daily". However, Paul never once in his teaching, did he say that we must die to self, daily. Paul was left for dead a few times, shipwrecked a few times and many people wanted and tried to kill him from city to city. He had a death warrant on him and in his writing, he said I die daily. Yet somehow from three words a whole teaching has come out of It, meaning something that Paul himself never taught. He taught many times about living by the Holy Spirit. Although we have been taught in the Bible about putting off the deeds of darkness. There is a difference between putting off t bad deeds and the thinking of dying to self. To put of bad deeds is to say my deeds are bad, but to die to self is to say that I am bad. Yet clearly the teaching from the Bible to Christians is we are new creations in Christ. Our spirit man in Christ is right before God. The teaching of death to self has left believers seeing themselves as bad before God. What father wants his child to die to self? The Church would give off at others for believing that during communion that Jesus dies again and again, since we know that Jesus died once and for all and never to be done again. Yet the same Bible that says Jesus died once and for all is the same Bible that says he was crucified with Christ. So, the idea of us having to die to self-daily is crazy. Read Galations 2:20 and Romans 6:6.

So, Jesus died once and for all and we were crucified with him, and that too should mean once and for all. So, it's just old thinking and bad deeds that needs to be put away. Also, the people that seek to "die to self" seem always to be relying on their best efforts. The first man to teach me about dying to self said, that to die to self was the main thing as a Christian. He seemed to be very stressful and burned out as he was typing out a sermon for his minister to be read out on a Sunday. His minister had it easy as the sermon was typed out for him. But there was nothing to do with relying on the Holy Spirit in what they did. I even hear a very popular minister say that both God and the devil are trying to kill him. Which Bible does people read? Clearly in John 10:10

it's only the devil who wants to kill us and it is Jesus that wants to bring us life and the life in abundance. What part of this do people not understand? We may need pruned at times but dying to self-teaching brings an idea of unworthiness to people before God, as they are not dead yet. It is another unbiblical teaching of dead works in striving to please God with self-efforts. Bad teaching has an effect on people's faith and therefore their prayer life. Then we wonder why it seems dead too often in prayer meetings. Maybe if they realised that God does not want them to die daily but live daily, and he loves them that the prayer life in many will change also.

Romans 8:13 lets us know it's by the spirit that we put up the DEEDS of the flesh. And Galatians 5;16 lets us know that "if we live by the Spirit that we won't live by the flesh."

So instead of believing in Churchianity about dying to oneself daily, How about believing in Christianity in living daily by the Holy Spirit; while putting to death bad deeds. The Bible says my people perish for lack of knowledge Hosea 4:6.

Chapter 20

The teaching of under both law and grace.

Another popular teaching in church is believing, we are both under law and grace. Under the law even Moses (the humblest man on earth) hadn't got confidence before God at times. Many Christians believe we are under parts of law of the Jewish covenant. Teachers of grace believe we are right with God through faith in Jesus alone. The believers who think they are under both law and grace, accuse teachers of grace alone as giving people a licence to sin, yet I personally have never heard a teacher of grace say it's okay to sin. If I was to stick up for a teacher of grace, the law lovers would never give me a few seconds to hear me out. But would in there hard-hearted pride walks away without any dialogue? Preachers teach loads and we are under grace and law. One would say we aren't under law, but we are to live by the law. Yet just like much other teaching, I heard a preacher get one verse out of the BBible to try and justify his under-law teaching. After just one verse he came up with, he had loads of opinions (Churchianity) and a few beliefs from his Jewish friend to try back up his teaching. No one was ever built up in their faith in hearing this. So, one day I was given a chance to teach. I taught we were under grace and not law. But the way I did it was I got verse after verse chapter after chapter and book after book, reading out what the Bible says clearly without my opinion (Christianity). You would think it's clear as to what teaching of us both was biblically accurate. And again, the believers of under both law and grace never seem to believe that God is pleased with them in Christ. As for those who can't believe both. They always seem to be fearful and insecure. And too often believing that God is disappointed with us. Doom and gloom, and killjoys. I have seen believers go down this road of under law and grace, and over time their joy and love for life goes away. Even their physical and mental health deteriorates. Ministers that believe we are under both grace and law so much that they make up many more laws and rules of their own. Very moral in ways but so little joy or love. They always try to be good enough to earn or qualify for God's grace via laws and rules keeping. The same folks seem to be barren in getting answers to prayer or any evidence of the grace of God in their life. Loads of striving and efforts, with little results. Plus, their prayers are joyless and lifeless. Again, you would think it is simple to tell what teaching is more biblically accurate.

I am not saying I am the only one that prays like a Christian, but I will say there is not enough who pray as Christians out of the many that I know in my country. To pray as a Christian, we must honour God and his word that depends on the Holy Spirit, and the result is Christian prayer. But if we don't, then he won't. God will not honour fleshy good intentions, or any prayer that is of unbelief, double mindedness, man pleasing, or praying just to be heard. Imagine if all of the Churches started praying as Christians! To do so they have to come to God as God, honour and fear him his name and his word, more than fellow believers including leadership and rich folk. Imagine if they all believed they are who the Bible says they are and not demonic religion lies. Imagine if we put love God with everything and others as ourselves, as the most important thing, even more important than not smoking, not drinking or not smiling. Believing that God deeply loves us, and he wants to communicate with us as he did with Adam in the cool of the day. Imagine if they really believed the Bible more than denomination. Imagine stopping ticking each other's boxes and starting to honour God, knowing we will be held accountable as we pray also. Imagine folk stop waiting on others to honour God like this first, but be willing to do it even if you are the only one and get trouble or the cold shoulder for doing so. Then if people will honour God and his covenant, then he will make them joyful in the house of prayer. It sounds like good news and it is, but sadly it is popular in the dark. Folks are happy enough with Churchianity, a limited mixed version of Christianity. But it is Jesus who died for me and who I must give an account to. I hope others waken up to this also. I can be too easy to deceive ourselves at times in making excuses for wanting to please another person or people more than God. Admitting this to God will be a great help. When critical changes are needed, then the truth to bring the change will seem critical. The biggest problem to stopping understanding is not ignorance, as it can be open to learning, but rather the biggest problem to understanding is misunderstanding. With pride, thinking you know better, it will be near impossible to learn. Just like in the Bible when some religious folk who thought they knew who Jesus was, seems to be the ones who could not see or believe Jesus for who he truly is. It is hard to love someone whom you misunderstand.

In our blind spots that most of us have, Jesus had ways to show this. A prophet brought a parable to King David about an evil shepherd, but it was to help him see his own blind spot. The truth would have hurt David, but it brought him to repent of his major problem and see it for what it was, and to have a change of heart. Because of whom Jesus is and what he did on our behalf on the cross, and because we were crucified with him, we have our acceptance in him before God the father. We can now come to God in that truth alone and not because of our own humility, reverence or good works. All glory to God alone. May there be a stop to praying performance prayers, and a desire to pray prophetic prayers like in the psalms. One thing about the prayers in the psalms is the genuineness of the person praying and his openness of heart before God including the persons own weaknesses. Yet many times in the psalms does God replied back if they connect to the heart of God and see things from a different perspective. How much more should we be able to hear from God in the new covenant? Most will know that walking carelessly is sin, having unforgiveness, and unbelief will hinder a good prayer life. Yet what can hinder us the most and go unnoticed is superstition.

I remember very early in my Christian faith that God convicted me for I was superstitious in prayer. I found this hard to believe as I never liked superstitious stuff all my life. God convicted me that my "prayers" was not much different from a person touching wood or crossing fingers for good luck. And that in prayer I was just saying the right words in prayer out of routine and not truly mindful or conscious of God at all. Thinking that by saying these prayers the day will go better, and if I don't say my prayers than the day will be bad. But that is trusting in the prayer itself rather than in God. Still to this day it can be a factor in my life that to easily creep back. That time when God was telling me this, I was already saying my "prayers" and I could tell God was looking to speak to me, but I felt interrupted by God and I was hoping for God to wait until I finished my "prayers" before he interrupted me further! But God was interrupting me again and I remember me saying to God "can't you see that I am praying". Then a realisation came to me that what I thought was the way to pray was wrong, and that praying is supposed to be communication with God first and foremost. Then I questioned myself if that is real prayer, then what was that saying "prayers" all about that I was doing? I had to stop saying "prayers" if I wanted to pray. It was pure spiritual junk that fooled me and was probably the biggest hindrance in my Christian faith. I would also say is in most others faith. I thought I was doing good as I sounded just like the church folk, but not like in the bible folk. Even lately I have been trying too hard in prayers, in order to make it dramatic and powerful, trying to force it too much. So, for me it's time to trip things back a little and be more genuine and not try to be too spiritual either. In prayer it can be like seasons as it changes how it goes. For weeks it can be more joyful, then for days it can be more a time for me to listen, a time to hear from God more and a time for me to open my heart to God about all my fears and cares. I believe we hear God more often than we realise as when we get an answer it can be for us to do something outside of our comfort zone. As fear normally screams in our heads, yet the word of God normally comes in still a small voice.

I had to give up on my way of praying to do it God's way, and the same goes for everyone. Other superstitious ways of praying are believing that if they pray sounding "spiritual" like praying in an old man's voice, praying in old English language, praying loud, quiet, long, and forceful or even with false humility. Our God and father of our Lord

Jesus Christ does not need or want fake in our praying. Its form of pride doing it our own performance way, just like Cain with his performance works that was rejected by God. He must have believed he was going to impress God. It surely must have seemed right to him. At times it is easily to think prayer is more depending on our efforts and we take ourselves too seriously to the point we become uptight. That's how superstitious pride can make us think. It seems needful to have a detox now and again from religious superstitions. Yet warning against superstitions is never unheard of in church, they think it's just others that can have it like people how bow to religious statues, crossing fingers or touching wood for luck. Yet superstition goes un-noticed while it plays such a big major role wrongfully within churches and our personal lives. In prayer God doesn't need our help, we need his. But how beautiful and wonderful prayer can and will be as a Christian once we detox ourselves from Churchianity. There are many religions around the world that pray with good intentions and best efforts, yet with no connection with God. Jesus along is the way. Good intentions and best efforts do not mean pleasing with God just because you say you are a Christian? Sadly, I heard some cults use the church type of praying of an example of how not to pray using repetitive prayers. Even cults won't do the repetitive stuff! The cults will say pray to God from the heart, though that sounds good, it isn't enough if it doesn't believe that Jesus Christ is Lord. Churchianity is a disconnected gospel. It makes it clear that we will all meet God and go to heaven or hell when we die, but it fails to understand our connection with God through Christ. The idea of peace with God, right with God or even saved seems to mean it will be okay for us when we die and we will go to heaven. Yet at the same time the truth that they have peace with God now here seems hard to believe and take in, as it goes against wrong beliefs. Being born again they know is needed to get into heaven, but Jesus didn't say get born again just to get into heaven when you die. Jesus said unless a man is born again, he will not see the kingdom of God. The kingdom of God is at hand, and even within the believer hear and now. If you cannot see the kingdom of God is here at least in part, then are you truly born again? The born- again gospel of the Lord Jesus Christ is not a disconnected gospel. That is why not only is prayer something that folk want to send to God in Jesus name, but even preachers of the gospel seem to talk only of God as a big distance angry man with no personal connection. Yes, Jesus did warn of hell and want people in heaven, but he also preached on abiding in him, being one in him as he is with the Father here on earth now. It is not the word hell that people fear but disconnectedness and loneliness, not fitting in and belonging. To most not fitting in is hell on earth. Maybe if they realised hell is the worst for being all along. If they knew that faith in Christ means being truly connected with God here and now, and not just when you die, then that would help change things. Jesus said that signs and wonders would follow the preaching of the gospel, if there is no signs and wonders following then is it truly the gospel that is preached?

When Paul the Apostle said he counted all things as dung that he may gain Christ, he was talking about his old religious ways. If many people want to gain more of the reality of Christ in their lives, then they will need to do the same thing. They may have giving up some bad habits and bad morals, but will they give up Churchianity? Jesus is worthy of our hearts for him, and is much more rewarding than dead religion. May God awaken us up, amen.

Lightning Source UK Ltd.
Milton Keynes UK
UKHW020805160921
390679UK00003B/351